THE CHRYSOSTOM BIBLE
A Commentary Series for Preaching and Teaching
The Pastorals: A Commentary

THE CHRYSOSTOM BIBLE
A Commentary Series for Preaching and Teaching

The Pastorals: A Commentary

Paul Nadim Tarazi

OCABS PRESS
ST PAUL, MINNESOTA 55124
2016

In memory of
Ralph Sergi

THE CHRYSOSTOM BIBLE
THE PASTORALS: A COMMENTARY

Copyright © 2016 by
Paul Nadim Tarazi

ISBN 1-60191-033-9

All rights reserved.

PRINTED IN THE UNITED STATES OF AMERICA

Other Books by the Author

I Thessalonians: A Commentary

Galatians: A Commentary

The Old Testament: An Introduction

Volume 1: Historical Traditions, revised edition

Volume 2: Prophetic Traditions

Volume 3: Psalms and Wisdom

The New Testament: An Introduction

Volume 1: Paul and Mark

Volume 2: Luke and Acts

Volume 3: Johannine Writings

Volume 4: Matthew and the Canon

The Chrysostom Bible

Genesis: A Commentary

Philippians: A Commentary

Romans: A Commentary

Colossians & Philemon: A Commentary

1 Corinthians: A Commentary

Ezekiel: A Commentary

Joshua: A Commentary

2 Corinthians: A Commentary

Isaiah: A Commentary

Jeremiah: A Commentary

Hebrews: A Commentary

Land and Covenant

The Chrysostom Bible
The Pastorals: A Commentary

Copyright © 2016 by Paul Nadim Tarazi
All rights reserved.

ISBN 1-60191-033-9

Published by OCABS Press, St. Paul, Minnesota.
Printed in the United States of America.

Books are available through OCABS Press at special discounts for bulk purchases in the United States by academic institutions, churches, and other organizations. For more information please email OCABS Press at press@ocabs.org.

Abbreviations

Books by the Author

1 Thess	*1 Thessalonians: A Commentary,* Crestwood, NY: St. Vladimir's Seminary Press, 1982
Gal	*Galatians: A Commentary,* Crestwood, NY: St. Vladimir's Seminary Press, 1994
OTI$_1$	*The Old Testament: An Introduction, Volume 1: Historical Traditions,* revised edition, Crestwood, NY: St. Vladimir's Seminary Press, 2003
OTI$_2$	*The Old Testament: An Introduction, Volume 2: Prophetic Traditions,* Crestwood, NY: St. Vladimir's Seminary Press, 1994
OTI$_3$	*The Old Testament: An Introduction, Volume 3: Psalms and Wisdom,* Crestwood, NY: St. Vladimir's Seminary Press, 1996
NTI$_1$	*The New Testament: An Introduction, Volume 1: Paul and Mark,* Crestwood, NY: St. Vladimir's Seminary Press, 1999
NTI$_2$	*The New Testament: An Introduction, Volume 2: Luke and Acts,* Crestwood, NY: St. Vladimir's Seminary Press, 2001
NTI$_3$	*The New Testament: An Introduction, Volume 3: Johannine Writings,* Crestwood, NY: St. Vladimir's Seminary Press, 2004
NTI$_4$	*The New Testament: An Introduction, Volume 4: Matthew and the Canon,* St. Paul, MN: OCABS Press, 2009
C-Gen	*Genesis: A Commentary.* The Chrysostom Bible. St. Paul, MN: OCABS Press, 2009
C-Phil	*Philippians: A Commentary.* The Chrysostom Bible. St. Paul, MN: OCABS Press, 2009
C-Rom	*Romans: A Commentary.* The Chrysostom Bible. St. Paul, MN: OCABS Press, 2010
C-Col	*Colossians & Philemon: A Commentary.* The Chrysostom Bible. St. Paul, MN: OCABS Press, 2010
C-1Cor	*1 Corinthians: A Commentary.* The Chrysostom Bible. St. Paul, MN: OCABS Press, 2011
C-Ezek	*Ezekiel: A Commentary.* The Chrysostom Bible. St. Paul, MN: OCABS Press, 2012
C-Josh	*Joshua: A Commentary.* The Chrysostom Bible. St. Paul, MN: OCABS Press, 2013
C-2Cor	*2 Corinthians: A Commentary.* The Chrysostom Bible. St. Paul, MN: OCABS Press, 2013

C-Is	*Isaiah: A Commentary.* The Chrysostom Bible. St. Paul, MN: OCABS Press, 2013
C-Jer	*Jeremiah: A Commentary.* The Chrysostom Bible. St. Paul, MN: OCABS Press, 2013
C-Heb	*Hebrews: A Commentary.* The Chrysostom Bible. St. Paul, MN: OCABS Press, 2014
LAC	*Land and Covenant,* St. Paul, MN: OCABS Press, 2009

Abbreviations

Books of the Old Testament*

Gen	Genesis	Job	Job	Hab		Habakkuk
Ex	Exodus	Ps	Psalms	Zeph		Zephaniah
Lev	Leviticus	Prov	Proverbs	Hag		Haggai
Num	Numbers	Eccl	Ecclesiastes	Zech		Zechariah
Deut	Deuteronomy	Song	Song of Solomon	Mal		Malachi
Josh	Joshua	Is	Isaiah	Tob		Tobit
Judg	Judges	Jer	Jeremiah	Jdt		Judith
Ruth	Ruth	Lam	Lamentations	Wis		Wisdom
1 Sam	1 Samuel	Ezek	Ezekiel	Sir		Sirach (Ecclesiasticus)
2 Sam	2 Samuel	Dan	Daniel	Bar		Baruch
1 Kg	1 Kings	Hos	Hosea	1 Esd		1 Esdras
2 Kg	2 Kings	Joel	Joel	2 Esd		2 Esdras
1 Chr	1 Chronicles	Am	Amos	1 Macc		1 Maccabees
2 Chr	2 Chronicles	Ob	Obadiah	2 Macc		2 Maccabees
Ezra	Ezra	Jon	Jonah	3 Macc		3 Maccabees
Neh	Nehemiah	Mic	Micah	4 Macc		4 Maccabees
Esth	Esther	Nah	Nahum			

Books of the New Testament

Mt	Matthew	Eph	Ephesians	Heb		Hebrews
Mk	Mark	Phil	Philippians	Jas		James
Lk	Luke	Col	Colossians	1 Pet		1 Peter
Jn	John	1 Thess	1 Thessalonians	2 Pet		2 Peter
Acts	Acts	2 Thess	2 Thessalonians	1 Jn		1 John
Rom	Romans	1 Tim	1 Timothy	2 Jn		2 John
1 Cor	1 Corinthians	2 Tim	2 Timothy	3 Jn		3 John
2 Cor	2 Corinthians	Titus	Titus	Jude		Jude
Gal	Galatians	Philem	Philemon	Rev		Revelation

*Following the larger canon known as the Septuagint.

Contents

Preface	*17*
Introduction	*21*
1 Timothy	
Chapter 1	*27*
Chapter 2	*45*
Chapter 3	*55*
Chapter 4	*67*
Chapter 5	*77*
Chapter 6	*87*
Tradition and Deposit	*101*
Absenteeism versus Divine Invisibility	*105*
2 Timothy	
Chapter 1	*117*
Chapter 2	*133*
Chapter 3	*141*
Jannes and Jambres	*147*
Chapter 4	*151*
Titus	
Chapter 1	*169*
Chapter 2	*183*
Chapter 3	*189*
Further Reading	*199*
Commentaries and Studies	*199*
Articles	*200*

Preface

The present Bible Commentary Series is not so much in honor of John Chrysostom as it is to continue and promote his legacy as an interpreter of the biblical texts for preaching and teaching God's congregation, in order to prod its members to proceed on the way they started when they accepted God's calling. Chrysostom's virtual uniqueness is that he did not subscribe to any hermeneutic or methodology, since this would amount to introducing an extra-textual authority over the biblical texts. For him, scripture is its own interpreter. Listening to the texts time and again allowed him to realize that "call" and "read (aloud)" are not interconnected realities; rather, they are one reality since they both are renditions of the same Hebrew verb *qara'*. Given that words read aloud are words of instruction for one "to do them," the only valid reaction would be to hear, listen, obey, and abide by these words. All these connotations are subsumed in the same Hebrew verb *šamaʻ*. On the other hand, these scriptural "words of life" are presented as readily understandable utterances of a father to his children (Isaiah 1:2-3). The recipients are never asked to engage in an intellectual debate with their divine instructor, or even among themselves, to fathom what he is saying. The Apostle to the Gentiles followed in the footsteps of the Prophets to Israel by handing down to them the Gospel, that is, the Law of God's Spirit through his Christ (Romans 8:2; Galatians 6:2) as fatherly instruction (1 Corinthians 4:15). He in turn wrote readily understandable letters to be read aloud. It is in these same footsteps that Chrysostom followed, having learned from both the Prophets and Paul that the same "words of life" carry also the sentence of death at the hand of the scriptural God, Judge of all (Deuteronomy 28; Joshua 8:32-35; Psalm 82; Matthew 3:4-12; Romans 2:12-16; 1 Corinthians 10:1-11; Revelation 20:11-15).

While theological debates and hermeneutical theories come and go after having fed their proponents and their fans with passing human glory, the Golden Mouth's expository homilies, through the centuries, fed and still feed myriads of believers in so many traditions and countries. Virtually banned from dogmatic treatises, he survives in the hearts of "those who have ears to hear." His success is due to his commitment to exegesis rather than to futile hermeneutics. The latter behaves as someone who dictates on a living organism what it is supposed to be, whereas exegesis submits to that organism and endeavors to decipher it through trial and error. There is as much a far cry between the text and the theories about it as there is between a living organism and the theories about it. The biblical texts are the reality of God imparted through their being read aloud in the midst of the congregation, disregarding the value of the sermon that follows. The sermon, much less a theological treatise, is at best an invitation to hear and obey the text. Assessing the shape of an invitation card has no value whatsoever when it comes to the dinner itself; the guests are fed by the dinner, not by the invitation or its phrasing (Luke 14:16-24; Matthew 22:1-14).

This commentary series does not intend to promote Chrysostom's ideas as a public relation manager would do, but rather to follow in the footsteps of his approach as true children and heirs are expected to do. He used all the contemporary tools at his disposal to communicate God's written instruction to his hearers, as a doctor would with his patients, without spending unnecessary energy on peripheral debates requiring the use of professional jargon incomprehensible to the commoner. The writers of this series will try to do the same: muster to the best of their ability all necessary contemporary knowledge to communicate to the general readers the biblical message without burdening them with data unnecessary for that purpose. Whenever it will be deemed necessary or even helpful to do so, and in order to curtail burdensome and lengthy technical asides within the commentaries, specialized monographs related either to specific topics or to the scriptural background—literary, socio-political, or archeological—will be issued as companions to the series.

Paul Nadim Tarazi
Editor

Introduction

Just as the two letters to the Corinthians and the two letters to the Thessalonians form a pair to be read in tandem, so are the two letters to Timothy. This is evident in the similar phraseology in the opening of each of the double letters:

> Paul, called by the will of God to be an apostle of Christ Jesus, and our brother Sosthenes, to the church of God which is at Corinth, to those sanctified in Christ Jesus, called to be saints together with all those who in every place call on the name of our Lord Jesus Christ, both their Lord and ours. (1 Cor 1:1-2)

> Paul, an apostle of Christ Jesus by the will of God, and Timothy our brother, to the church of God which is at Corinth, with all the saints who are in the whole of Achaia. (2 Cor 1:1)

> Paul, Silvanus, and Timothy, to the church of the Thessalonians in God the Father and the Lord Jesus Christ: Grace to you and peace. We give thanks to God always for you all, constantly mentioning you in our prayers, remembering before our God and Father your work of faith and labor of love and steadfastness of hope in our Lord Jesus Christ. (1 Thess 1:1-3)

> Paul, Silvanus, and Timothy, to the church of the Thessalonians in God our Father and the Lord Jesus Christ: Grace to you and peace from God the Father and the Lord Jesus Christ. We are bound to give thanks to God always for you, brethren, as is fitting, because your faith is growing abundantly, and the love of every one of you for one another is increasing. (2 Thess 1:1-3)

> Paul, an apostle of Christ Jesus by command of God our Savior and of Christ Jesus our hope, to Timothy, my true child in the faith: Grace, mercy, and peace from God the Father and Christ Jesus our Lord. (1 Tim 1:1-2)

> Paul, an apostle of Christ Jesus by the will of God according to the promise of the life which is in Christ Jesus, to Timothy, my beloved

child: Grace, mercy, and peace from God the Father and Christ Jesus our Lord. (2 Tim 1:1-2)

In the Pastoral Letters, one would have expected that either "office of bishop" (*episkopēs*) or "bishop" (*episkopon*) that occur in tandem in 1 Timothy 3:1-2 would be used in 2 Timothy. Yet, it is in Titus that one hears of the qualifications of a bishop in a passage that closely parallels the one found in 1 Timothy:

> Now a bishop must be above reproach, the husband of one wife, temperate, sensible, dignified, hospitable, an apt teacher, no drunkard, not violent but gentle, not quarrelsome, and no lover of money. He must manage his own household well, keeping his children submissive and respectful in every way; for if a man does not know how to manage his own household, how can he care for God's church? (1Tim 3:2-5)

> For a bishop, as God's steward, must be blameless; he must not be arrogant or quick-tempered or a drunkard or violent or greedy for gain, but hospitable, a lover of goodness, master of himself, upright, holy, and self-controlled; he must hold firm to the sure word as taught, so that he may be able to give instruction in sound doctrine and also to confute those who contradict it. (Tit 1:7-9)

Consequently, the author intended that all three letters be read as one unit, just as is the case with the three letters of John.[1] What is their combined message when taken together?

As I shall discuss in more detail in the commentary one striking feature of the Pastoral Letters is the total absence of the verb *paradidōmi* (deliver)[2] and its cognate *paradosis* (tradition). Instead, the verb *paratithemai* (entrust as deposit) and its cognate *paratēkē* (deposit) are used to emphasize that what is written is not to be interpreted subjectively, nor is it to be modified, changed, or

---

[1] See my comments in *NTI₃* 269-70.
[2] Except as an apostolic prerogative: "… among them Hymenaeus and Alexander, whom I have delivered (*paredōka*) to Satan that they may learn not to blaspheme." (1Tim 1:20)

developed in any way. Still, the verb *paratithemai* and its cognate noun *parathēkē* are nowhere to be found in Titus. One gets the distinct impression that the bishop of Crete is not entrusted with the deposit as is Timothy, the bishop of Ephesus—the Pauline headquarters. This impression turns into certitude when, at the end of 2 Timothy, one hears Paul saying: "For Demas, in love with this present world, has deserted me and gone to Thessalonica; Crescens has gone to Galatia, Titus to Dalmatia." (2 Tim 4:10) Conversely, Paul's decision to assign Titus to the far off island of Crete exudes a sense of judgment, or at least a last test, given that the original Greek name of the island is *Krētēs* which sounds similar to *kritēs* (judge). The intended lesson is the same found in Romans 11 where the Gentiles are forewarned not be puffed up lest they too fall as the Jews before them did. And here, in the third Pastoral Letter, we hear of the prime Gentile Titus who accompanied Paul to the meeting at Jerusalem as showcase (Gal 2:1-3) is not exempt of such. So Gentiles, beware! This caveat sounds actually more ominous than that in Romans since it is Paul's last call. Prefacing his reference to Titus' desertion (2 Tim 4:10) Paul bids Timothy his last farewell in these terms:

> For I am already on the point of being sacrificed; the time of my departure has come. I have fought the good fight, I have finished the race, I have kept the faith. Henceforth there is laid up for me the crown of righteousness, which the Lord, the righteous judge (*kritēs*), will award to me on that Day, and not only to me but also to all who have loved his appearing. Do your best to come to me soon. (vv.6-9)

1 Timothy

Chapter 1

Vv. 1:20 ¹Παῦλος ἀπόστολος Χριστοῦ Ἰησοῦ κατ' ἐπιταγὴν θεοῦ σωτῆρος ἡμῶν καὶ Χριστοῦ Ἰησοῦ τῆς ἐλπίδος ἡμῶν ²Τιμοθέῳ γνησίῳ τέκνῳ ἐν πίστει, χάρις ἔλεος εἰρήνη ἀπὸ θεοῦ πατρὸς καὶ Χριστοῦ Ἰησοῦ τοῦ κυρίου ἡμῶν. ³Καθὼς παρεκάλεσά σε προσμεῖναι ἐν Ἐφέσῳ πορευόμενος εἰς Μακεδονίαν, ἵνα παραγγείλῃς τισὶν μὴ ἑτεροδιδασκαλεῖν ⁴μηδὲ προσέχειν μύθοις καὶ γενεαλογίαις ἀπεράντοις, αἵτινες ἐκζητήσεις παρέχουσιν μᾶλλον ἢ οἰκονομίαν θεοῦ τὴν ἐν πίστει. ⁵τὸ δὲ τέλος τῆς παραγγελίας ἐστὶν ἀγάπη ἐκ καθαρᾶς καρδίας καὶ συνειδήσεως ἀγαθῆς καὶ πίστεως ἀνυποκρίτου, ⁶ὧν τινες ἀστοχήσαντες ἐξετράπησαν εἰς ματαιολογίαν ⁷θέλοντες εἶναι νομοδιδάσκαλοι, μὴ νοοῦντες μήτε ἃ λέγουσιν μήτε περὶ τίνων διαβεβαιοῦνται. ⁸Οἴδαμεν δὲ ὅτι καλὸς ὁ νόμος, ἐάν τις αὐτῷ νομίμως χρῆται, ⁹εἰδὼς τοῦτο, ὅτι δικαίῳ νόμος οὐ κεῖται, ἀνόμοις δὲ καὶ ἀνυποτάκτοις, ἀσεβέσι καὶ ἁμαρτωλοῖς, ἀνοσίοις καὶ βεβήλοις, πατρολῴαις καὶ μητρολῴαις, ἀνδροφόνοις ¹⁰πόρνοις ἀρσενοκοίταις ἀνδραποδισταῖς ψεύσταις ἐπιόρκοις, καὶ εἴ τι ἕτερον τῇ ὑγιαινούσῃ διδασκαλίᾳ ἀντίκειται ¹¹κατὰ τὸ εὐαγγέλιον τῆς δόξης τοῦ μακαρίου θεοῦ, ὃ ἐπιστεύθην ἐγώ. ¹²Χάριν ἔχω τῷ ἐνδυναμώσαντί με Χριστῷ Ἰησοῦ τῷ κυρίῳ ἡμῶν, ὅτι πιστόν με ἡγήσατο θέμενος εἰς διακονίαν ¹³τὸ πρότερον ὄντα βλάσφημον καὶ διώκτην καὶ ὑβριστήν, ἀλλὰ ἠλεήθην, ὅτι ἀγνοῶν ἐποίησα ἐν ἀπιστίᾳ· ¹⁴ὑπερεπλεόνασεν δὲ ἡ χάρις τοῦ κυρίου ἡμῶν μετὰ πίστεως καὶ ἀγάπης τῆς ἐν Χριστῷ Ἰησοῦ. ¹⁵πιστὸς ὁ λόγος καὶ πάσης ἀποδοχῆς ἄξιος, ὅτι Χριστὸς Ἰησοῦς ἦλθεν εἰς τὸν κόσμον ἁμαρτωλοὺς σῶσαι, ὧν πρῶτός εἰμι ἐγώ. ¹⁶ἀλλὰ διὰ τοῦτο ἠλεήθην, ἵνα ἐν ἐμοὶ πρώτῳ ἐνδείξηται Χριστὸς Ἰησοῦς τὴν ἅπασαν μακροθυμίαν πρὸς ὑποτύπωσιν τῶν μελλόντων πιστεύειν ἐπ' αὐτῷ εἰς ζωὴν αἰώνιον. ¹⁷Τῷ δὲ βασιλεῖ τῶν αἰώνων, ἀφθάρτῳ ἀοράτῳ μόνῳ θεῷ, τιμὴ καὶ δόξα εἰς τοὺς αἰῶνας τῶν αἰώνων, ἀμήν. ¹⁸Ταύτην τὴν παραγγελίαν παρατίθεμαί σοι, τέκνον Τιμόθεε, κατὰ τὰς προαγούσας ἐπὶ σὲ προφητείας, ἵνα στρατεύῃ ἐν αὐταῖς τὴν καλὴν στρατείαν ¹⁹ἔχων πίστιν καὶ ἀγαθὴν συνείδησιν, ἥν τινες ἀπωσάμενοι περὶ τὴν πίστιν ἐναυάγησαν, ²⁰ὧν ἐστιν Ὑμέναιος καὶ Ἀλέξανδρος, οὓς παρέδωκα τῷ σατανᾷ, ἵνα παιδευθῶσιν μὴ βλασφημεῖν.

¹Paul, an apostle of Christ Jesus by command of God our Savior and of Christ Jesus our hope, ²To Timothy, my true child in the faith: Grace, mercy, and peace from God the Father and Christ Jesus our Lord. ³As I urged you when I was going to Macedonia, remain at Ephesus that you may charge certain persons not to teach any different doctrine, ⁴nor to occupy themselves with myths and endless genealogies which promote speculations rather than the divine training that is in faith; ⁵whereas the aim of our charge is love that issues from a pure heart and a good conscience and sincere faith. ⁶Certain persons by swerving from these have wandered away into vain discussion, ⁷desiring to be teachers of the law, without understanding either what they are saying or the things about which they make assertions. ⁸Now we know that the law is good, if any one uses it lawfully,⁹ understanding this, that the law is not laid down for the just but for the lawless and disobedient, for the ungodly and sinners, for the unholy and profane, for murderers of fathers and murderers of mothers, for manslayers, ¹⁰immoral persons, sodomites, kidnapers, liars, perjurers, and whatever else is contrary to sound doctrine, ¹¹in accordance with the glorious gospel of the blessed God with which I have been entrusted. ¹²I thank him who has given me strength for this, Christ Jesus our Lord, because he judged me faithful by appointing me to his service, ¹³though I formerly blasphemed and persecuted and insulted him; but I received mercy because I had acted ignorantly in unbelief, ¹⁴and the grace of our Lord overflowed for me with the faith and love that are in Christ Jesus. ¹⁵The saying is sure and worthy of full acceptance, that Christ Jesus came into the world to save sinners. And I am the foremost of sinners; ¹⁶but I received mercy for this reason, that in me, as the foremost, Jesus Christ might display his perfect patience for an example to those who were to believe in him for eternal

life. ¹⁷ To the King of ages, immortal, invisible, the only God, be honor and glory for ever and ever. Amen. ¹⁸ This charge I commit to you, Timothy, my son, in accordance with the prophetic utterances which pointed to you, that inspired by them you may wage the good warfare, ¹⁹ holding faith and a good conscience. By rejecting conscience, certain persons have made shipwreck of their faith, ²⁰ among them Hymenaeus and Alexander, whom I have delivered to Satan that they may learn not to blaspheme.

When dealing with the Pastoral Letters[1], it is the cumulative effect of the terminology on the hearers' ears, that is, the "managed itinerary" of that terminology, which gives the ultimate trajectory of the message.[2] Let us listen to the greetings of the three letters:

Paul, an apostle of Christ Jesus by command (*epitagēn*) of God our Savior and of Christ Jesus our *hope*, to Timothy, my true (*gnēsiō*) child in the *faith*: Grace, mercy, and peace from God the Father and Christ Jesus our Lord. (1 Tim 1:1-2)

Paul, an apostle of Christ Jesus by the will of God according to the *promise* of the *life* which is in Christ Jesus, to Timothy, my beloved child: Grace, mercy, and peace from God the Father and Christ Jesus our Lord. (2 Tim 1:1-2)

Paul, a servant (*doulos*; slave) of God and an apostle of Jesus Christ, to further the *faith* of God's elect and their knowledge of the truth which accords with godliness, in *hope* of eternal *life* which God, who never lies, *promised* ages ago and at the proper time manifested in his word through the preaching (*kērygmati*) with which I have been entrusted by command (*epitagēn*) of God our Savior, to Titus, my true (*gnēsiō*) child in a common *faith*: Grace and peace from God the Father and Christ Jesus our Savior. (Tit 1:1-4)

Even with a cursory reading, one can easily see that the last greeting sums up the first two greetings and incorporates into it

---

[1] 1 Timothy, 2 Timothy, Titus.
[2] See the discussion in the Introduction.

classic Pauline phraseology, including "servant," "God's elect," "knowledge of the truth," "manifested," "preaching" (*kērygmati*; heralding), "entrusted," "true child," and "godliness" (*evsebeian*).[3] The most noticeable feature of the third greeting is that it combines "hope" (1 Tim 1:1) and "promise of life" (2 Tim 1:1) into "hope of eternal life which God promised" (Tit 1:2).

Still, there is a very interesting progression between the first greeting and the last greeting that reflects a full grasp of the Pauline gospel. Though the second greeting uses the traditional Pauline phrase "apostle by the will (*dia thelēmatos*) of God," the first and third speak of Paul having been assigned to this position "by the command (*kat' epitagēn*) of God." This particular phraseology is used to underscore that the will of God is none other than that expressed in the Old Testament scripture. This same thought brackets Paul's letter to the Romans:

> Paul, a servant of Jesus Christ, called to be an apostle, set apart for the gospel of God which he *promised* beforehand through his prophets in the holy scriptures... (1:1-2)

> Now to him who is able to strengthen you according to my *gospel* and the preaching (*kērygmati*) of Jesus Christ, according to the revelation of the mystery which was kept secret for long ages (*khronois aiōniois*) but is now disclosed (*phanerōthentos*; manifested) and through the prophetic writings is made known (*gnōristhentos*) to all nations, according to the command (*kat' epitagēn*) of the eternal (*aiōniou*) God, to bring about the obedience of *faith*—to the only wise God be glory for evermore through Jesus Christ! Amen. (16:25-27)

The almost verbatim correspondence between the ending of Romans (16:25-27) and the opening of Titus is unmistakable:

---

[3] "Godliness" (*evsebeian*) is the opposite of "wickedness" (*asebeian*).

> Paul, a servant of God and an apostle of Jesus Christ, to further the *faith* of God's elect and their knowledge (*epignōsin*; from the same root as *gnōristhentos*) of the truth which accords with godliness, in hope of eternal (*aiōniou*) life which God, who never lies, promised ages ago (*pro khronōn aiōniōn*) and at the proper time manifested (*ephanerōsen*) in his word through the preaching (*kērygmati*) with which I have been entrusted by command (*epitagēn*) of God our Savior, to Titus, my true child in a common *faith*: Grace and peace from God the Father and Christ Jesus our Savior. (Tit 1:1-4)

That Romans was paramount on the author's mind is evidenced by the specific reference to God as the "savior." In the Pauline corpus this is found only in Romans and its twin letter, Philippians,[4] and no less in conjunction with the gospel:

> For I am not ashamed of the gospel: it is the power of God for salvation (*eis sōtērian*) to every one who has faith, to the Jew first and also to the Greek. (Rom 1:16)

> Brethren, my heart's desire and prayer to God for them is that they may be saved (*eis sōtērian*; for salvation). (10:1)

> Only let your manner of life be worthy of the gospel of Christ, so that whether I come and see you or am absent, I may hear of you that you stand firm in one spirit, with one mind striving side by side for the faith of the gospel, and not frightened in anything by your opponents (*antikeimenōn*). This is a clear omen to them of their destruction, but of your salvation, and that from God. (Phil 1:27-28)[5]

> Therefore, my beloved, as you have always obeyed, so now, not only as in my presence but much more in my absence, work out your

---

[4] See Philippians as mini-Romans in *C-Phil* 74, 113, 191, 192.
[5] The closeness with the Pastoral Letters can be further detected through the use of the Greek verb *antikeimai* (lie in opposition) used to describe the opponents of the gospel teaching. This verb occurs only four more times in the Pauline corpus, two of which in 1 Timothy (1 Cor 16:9; 2 Thess 2:4; 1 Tim 1:10; 5:14), and only twice more in Luke (13:17; 21:15).

own salvation with fear and trembling; for God is at work in you, both to will and to work for his good pleasure. (2:12-13)

By encircling the traditional introduction of Paul as "an apostle of Christ Jesus by the will of God" (2 Tim 1:2) within the double mention that he is so "by the command of God" (1 Tim 1:1; Tit 1:3), the author wanted to underline the primacy of the salvation of God presented in the Old Testament over the mission of Jesus Christ. It is through the agency of Paul that the message of salvation was shared with all nations. After having stressed that God is "the savior" (1 Tim 1:1; 2:3; 4:10), Jesus Christ is gradually introduced as also "the savior" (2 Tim 1:10; Tit 1:4; 2:13; 3:6) but without ever losing sight of the fact that God *remains* "the primary savior" (1:3; 2:10; 3:4). This priority of God over Jesus Christ is further evident in that after having twice presented Paul as "an apostle of Christ Jesus" (1 Tim 1:1; 2 Tim 1:1), there is a sudden switch to "a servant (*doulos*; slave) of God and an apostle of Jesus Christ" (Tit 1:1), which is unique phraseology in the New Testament.[6] What makes this combination even more stunning is that Paul has always spoken of himself as "servant" of "Jesus Christ," and never "of God."

Comparing the greetings in Timothy 1 and 2 with the greeting in Titus corroborates the movement toward God's supremacy, and is reflective of the coming judgment of both Jews and Gentiles in the light of the teaching of the Law that was shared with the nations through Paul's preaching (Rom 2:9-16). Timothy's "faith" (1 Tim 1:2; 2 Tim 1:5) becomes the "faith of God's elect" in Titus (1:1) and when attributed to Titus himself becomes the "common faith" (v.4). Further, in the letters to Timothy "mercy" is inserted between the classical Pauline "grace and peace" (1 Tim 1:2; 2 Tim 1:2), giving the hearers a double chance of mercy through divine "forbearance" (*makrothymia*; patience) before the

---

[6] The closest, yet not identical, phrase is "James, a servant (*doulos*; slave) of God and of the Lord Jesus Christ" (Jam 1:1).

final judgment. Such "mercy" is omitted in the letter to Titus thus evoking the idea of final judgment, which is expounded on in Romans:

> Therefore you have no excuse, O man, whoever you are, when you judge another; for in passing judgment upon him you condemn yourself, because you, the judge, are doing the very same things. We know that the judgment of God rightly falls upon those who do such things. Do you suppose, O man, that when you judge those who do such things and yet do them yourself, you will escape the judgment of God? Or do you presume upon the riches of his kindness and forbearance and patience (*makrothymias*)? Do you not know that God's kindness is meant to lead you to repentance? But by your hard and impenitent heart you are storing up wrath for yourself on the day of wrath when God's righteous judgment will be revealed. For he will render to every man according to his works: to those who by patience in well-doing seek for glory and honor and immortality, he will give eternal life; but for those who are factious and do not obey the truth, but obey wickedness, there will be wrath and fury. There will be tribulation and distress for every human being who does evil, the Jew first and also the Greek, but glory and honor and peace for every one who does good, the Jew first and also the Greek. For God shows no partiality. (Rom 2:1-11)

> > What if God, desiring to show his wrath and to make known his power, has endured with much patience (*makrothymia*) the vessels of wrath made for destruction, in order to make known the riches of his glory for the vessels of *mercy*, which he has prepared beforehand for glory, even us whom he has called, not from the Jews only but also from the Gentiles? (9:22-24)

The only way to avoid the divine "wrath and fury" is to repent by following the divine example and showing mercy unto others, just as Paul describes himself as having done:

I thank him who has given me strength for this, Christ Jesus our Lord, because he judged me faithful by appointing me to his service, though I formerly blasphemed and persecuted and insulted him; but I received mercy because I had acted ignorantly in unbelief, and the grace of our Lord overflowed for me with the faith and love that are in Christ Jesus. The saying (*logos*; word) is sure and worthy of full acceptance, that Christ Jesus came into the world to save sinners. And I am the foremost of sinners; but I received mercy for this reason, that in me, as the foremost, Jesus Christ might display his perfect patience for an example to those who were to believe in him for eternal life. To the King of ages, immortal, invisible, the only God, be honor and glory for ever and ever. Amen. (1 Tim 1:12-17)

This model of behavior is expressed throughout the Pastoral Letters. Forbearance (*makrothymia*; patience) is made part of the gospel word that is sure and worthy of acceptance, and is an integral part of the teaching Timothy is commissioned with: "preach (*kēryxon*; herald)[7] the word (*logon*), be urgent in season and out of season, convince, rebuke, and exhort, be unfailing in patience (*makrothymia*) and in teaching (*didakhē*)." (2 Tim 4:2)[8] From the beginning, Timothy's charge includes not only to remain faithful to Paul's teaching (*didaskalia*),[9] but also to mirror his patience: "As I urged you when I was going to Macedonia, remain at Ephesus that you may charge certain persons not to teach any different doctrine (*heterodidaskalein*)" (1 Tim 1:3); "Now you have observed my teaching (*didaskalia*), my conduct, my aim in life, my faith, my patience (*makrothymia*), my love, my steadfastness." (2 Tim 3:10)

---

[7] *kēryxon* is from the same root as *kērygma*, another classic Pauline term used to refer to the gospel.
[8] RSV waters down the intended impact of the original *logos*, a term tantamount to Paul's gospel in his letters.
[9] Both *didaskalia* and *didakhē* are from the same verbal root *didaskein*.

Timothy's charge is to begin by teaching the Old Testament scriptures, and to point out, as Paul did in Romans (7:12), "that the law (*nomos*) is good, if any one uses it lawfully (*nomimōs*)" (1 Tim 1:8). The entire passage (vv.3-11) is a compendium of the Pauline gospel expounded in Romans: the law is good *because* it is intended to reveal our misdeeds (1 Tim 1:8-11). It is not meant to promote self-righteousness under the pretext that it was entrusted to us (Rom 3:1), as Paul's opponents teach. Rather than occupying themselves with "divine training that is in faith" (1 Tim 1:4), such persons "have wandered away into vain discussion, desiring to be teachers of the law, without understanding either what they are saying or the things about which they make assertions" (1 Tim 1:6-7). Being aware of the law without doing its precepts is of no avail (Rom 2), and all those precepts are summed up in the love for the neighbor (13:8-10):

> As I urged you when I was going to Macedonia, remain at Ephesus that you may charge certain persons not to teach any different doctrine (*heterodidaskalein*), nor to occupy themselves with myths and endless genealogies which promote speculations rather than the divine training (*oikonomian*) that is in faith; whereas the aim of our charge is love that issues from a pure heart and a good conscience and sincere (*anypokritou*)[10] faith. (1 Tim 1:3-5)

Now that the Pauline gospel has been recapitulated, the charge to Timothy, the bishop of the Pauline headquarters in Ephesus, is to uphold this legacy. His instructions are articulated in three masterfully constructed verses (vv.18-20) using typical Pauline terminology. The first charge invokes the imagery of warfare: "... that inspired by them you may wage (*stratevē*) the good warfare (*strateian*)." (v.18). In Philippians, Timothy is introduced as Paul's "son" (*teknon*; 2:22; 1 Tim 1:2) just before Epahroditus,

---

[10] Compare with Romans where love is qualified as *anypokritos*: "Let love be genuine (*anypokritos*)" (12:9a). See also 2 Cor 6 where Paul refers to his apostolic "afflictions" that include "genuine (*anypokritō*) love" (v.6).

Timothy's successor, is qualified as Paul's "fellow soldier" (*systratiōtēn*; co-warrior, Phil 2:25). However, Timothy's assignment does not come from the Roman emperor or the governor of the province Asia, whose capital is Ephesus, but rather it is "according (*kata*) with the prophetic utterances" (1 Tim 1:18) of God the savior "according to whose command" (*kat' epitagēn*) Paul was designated apostle (v.1).

Nevertheless, there is an essential difference between God's relationship with Paul and that with Timothy. Paul's is a direct relationship (Gal 1:11-12). His main channel of communication with others is *paradosis* (tradition) from the verbal root *didōmi* (give, hand down). The "living" aspect of the *paradosis* is reflected in the "different" letters Paul wrote to "different" congregations. Timothy, however, is not an apostle, and thus he is not at liberty to do the same. What he received is handed down from Paul—not God—as *parathēkē* (deposit, from the verbal root *paratithēmi* [lay down]), and thus is an unchangeable "writ" to be preserved. That is why the New Testament canon does not contain any writ by Timothy. Paul's charge to Timothy is "committed" in the form of the two letters addressed to him: "This charge I commit (*paratithēmai*; entrust) to you (*soi*), Timothy, my son." (Tim 1:18a) *paratithēmai* is the middle voice of the verb *paratithēmi*, reflecting an action done for the sake of its agent. So, *paratithēmai soi* literally means "I entrust to your care something that is mine, for you to preserve for my sake." Consequently, Timothy has no choice but to abide *literally*—according to the *littera* (alphabetical letters) of the Pauline epistles—that is, by Paul's *written* bidding. This, in turn, clarifies the function of the example given of Hymenaeus and Alexander whom Paul "delivered to Satan" in Ephesus, just as he did the Corinthian man (1 Cor 5:5), so "that they may learn not to blaspheme" (1 Tim 1:20). Yet, they are no worse off than Paul himself who, because he "blasphemed" (v.13), "was given in the flesh a thorn, a messenger of Satan, to harass me, to keep him from being too elated" (2 Cor 12:7).

But who are Hymenaeus and Alexander? Besides Timothy and Pontius Pilate (1 Tim 6:13), these are the only personal names mentioned in this letter. In scripture, names of unknown persons cannot be accounted for unless they are taken metaphorically and thus make immediate sense functionally to the hearers in the context where they appear. Hymenaeus and Alexander are both Greek and thus Gentile names. Alexander, the easier understood and more readily recognized name, is used profusely in the New Testament. It unmistakably brings to mind Alexander of Macedon, the Hellene[11] who conquered Eastern Asia by the sword and prepared the way for the expansion of the Roman empire over those same regions. Just as with Caesar and Pontius Pilate, Alexander is representative of human power that subjugates others with the "sword," which is in total opposition to the gospel message whose power lies in the divine "word" of peace and reconciliation.[12] This understanding is confirmed in 2 Timothy 4:14-15, where Alexander is presented as a coppersmith (*khalkevs*), hence maker of swords and weapons in general: "Alexander the coppersmith (*khalkevs*) did me great harm; the Lord will requite him for his deeds. Beware of him yourself, for he strongly opposed our message."

Hymenaios (Hymenaeus) is an adjective formed from the noun *hymēn* (hymen), which is also the name of the Greek god of marriage, *Hymēn*. Although at face value its connotation is positive, Hymenaeus is presented in negative terms: "By rejecting conscience, certain persons have made shipwreck of their faith, among them Hymenaeus and Alexander, whom I have delivered to Satan that they may learn not to blaspheme." (1 Tim 1:19b-

---

[11] In the New Testament *hoi Hellēnes* (the Hellenes; the Greeks) and *ta ethnē* (the nations) are equivalent terms for the non-Jews. Although Alexander was Macedonian and fought first against the Greeks, he was not only a pupil of Aristotle, but he spread the Greek language throughout Eastern Asia, making of it the new *lingua franca* instead of Aramaic.

[12] See especially Rom 5:1-11 and Eph 6:13-17.

20) Just as in the case of Alexander, the negative connotation associated with Hymenaeus is revisited in 2 Timothy: "Avoid such godless chatter, for it will lead people into more and more ungodliness, and their talk will eat its way like gangrene. Among them are Hymenaeus and Philetus, who have swerved from the truth by holding that the resurrection is past already. They are upsetting the faith of some." (2:16-18)

In order to solve this apparent conundrum regarding the use of names and designations, it would be beneficial to delve into the function of *khalkevs* (2 Tim 4:14), especially since it is a unique occurrence in the New Testament. The oblique reference of coppersmith to the manufacture of weaponry, defensive as well as offensive, is corroborated in scripture itself. Three out of the four other instances of *khalkevs* occur in conjunction with the fabrication of idols (Is 41:7; 54:16; Sir 38:28). Its first mention is found as early as Genesis 4:22 in the larger context of Cain's lineage:

> Cain (*qayn*) knew his wife, and she conceived and bore Enoch; and he built a city, and called the name of the city after the name of his son, Enoch. To Enoch was born Irad; and Irad was the father of Mehujael, and Mehujael the father of Methushael, and Methushael the father of Lamech. And Lamech took two wives; the name of the one was Adah, and the name of the other Zillah. Adah bore Jabal; he was the father of those who dwell in tents and have cattle. His brother's name was Jubal; he was the father of all those who play the lyre and pipe. Zillah bore Tubal-cain; he was the forger (Greek *khalkevs*) of *all instruments of bronze and iron.* The sister of Tubal-cain (Hebrew *tubal-qayn*) was Naamah. Lamech said to his wives: "Adah and Zillah, hear my voice; you wives of Lamech, hearken to what I say: I have slain a man for wounding me, a young man for striking me. If Cain is avenged sevenfold, truly Lamech seventy-sevenfold." (Gen 4:17-24)

Looking closely at this genealogy, one will readily notice that it carries a double function. On the one hand, it shows that indeed God's blessing is still working in spite of man's misbehavior: "Cain knew his wife, and she conceived and bore Enoch" (4:17) just as "Adam knew Eve his wife, and she conceived and bore Cain" (v.1). On the other hand, the path chosen by man takes him farther away from the original setting of the garden where everything needed was provided by God and the little work man did was for enjoyment.[13] The path of man led to civilization whose most grandiose expression is the (imperial) city[14] that will ultimately stand arrogantly against God (11:1-9). It is as though factually Cain tried to circumvent God's decision to have him "dwell" in a "land of wandering" and decided instead to "dwell" in a city of his own making.

Eve's reaction to her having conceived and given birth is to acknowledge that the child is the gift of God rather than of her own making: "I have gotten a man with (the help of) the Lord." (4:1). In contrast to Eve's attitude of thanksgiving, Cain's reaction to his wife's giving birth was that he "built a city, and called the name of the city after the name of his son, Enoch." (v.17) The intended extreme irony can be seen in the name Enoch which is from the root *ḥnk* and has the connotation of "dedication."[15] Instead of taking his son's name seriously and dedicating him back to God, Cain makes his son, who is as much God's gift *as he himself is*, into a city. Cain, the man of (living) flesh, begets a man of (dead) stone! Instead of flesh formed through the blessing of procreation, Cain's legacy becomes, by choice, one of stone. This propensity, ultimately corrected by God at the end of the

---

[13] This is the meaning of the original *wayyaniḥehu* (and he made him relax) translated as "and he put him" (RSV; Gen 2:15). See my comments in *LAC* 32.
[14] Civilization and city are from the same root in the original Latin.
[15] *ḥanukkah* (Hanukkah), which is the Feast of the (Re)dedication of the Temple under the Maccabees, comes from the same root.

scriptural odyssey, is described in Ezekiel in terminology reminiscent of the first chapters of Genesis (Ezek 11:19-21; 18:31-32; 36:25-27).

In the meantime, this sad state of affairs is carried through until the seventh generation of Cain's progeny, that is, to its fullest extent, with God's approval and under his control.[16] As in Genesis 2 with the building of woman and in 1 Samuel 8 with the rise of kingship, God allows man's decision to take its course in order to show the hearers its calamitous end. The series of names in Cain's genealogy reflects that his progeny is furthering his way, that is, disregarding God's initial plan and following man's own will. The name of Enoch's son, Irad (*'irad*), is a combination of the noun *'ir* (city) and the verb *radah* (rule [over], have dominion [over]); thus the son of Enoch was to rule over the city named after his father.[17] The next in line is Mehujael (*meḥuya'el*) meaning "what he undertakes will be erased (they will erase)," and his son's name Methushael (*metuša'el*) means "what he asks for will die," reflecting the biblical end of the city (Samaria and Jerusalem). The name Lemech (*lemek*)[18] is a metathesis play on the Hebrew noun *melek* (king).[19] Two features related to Lemech corroborate this. First, he had more than one wife, which was a kingly prerogative,

---

[16] For the value of the numerical 7, see the Excursus on Number Symbolism in *NTI₃* 22-28. As for God's allowing events to happen against his express will, see Gen 2-3 and 1 Sam 8.

[17] *'irad* from *'ir-rad* without the repetition of the letter *r*. Keeping the final *h* of *radah* would have resulted in a feminine proper noun.

[18] Unfortunately the traditional English Lamech, starting with the King James Version, is incorrect. Lamech (*lāmek*) is found only in Gen 4:18. In the following four instances of the same name (vv.19, 23 [twice], 24) we have the Hebrew *lemek* (Lemech). This is repeated in Gen 5:25-31 where the first instance in v.25 is *lāmek* whereas the following four (vv.26, 28, 30, 31) are invariably *lemek*. The first instance in each passage is due to the fact that the personal noun is the last word of the verse. In this case, in Hebrew, we have what is called the pausal form where the vowel of the accented syllable in the word is lengthened, in this case from the short *e* to a long *ā*. A classic example of this rule is found in the very common noun *'ereṣ* (earth) that becomes *'āreṣ*.

[19] Metathesis is the switch between two consonants in the same word.

as one can see from the example of Saul (2 Sam 12:7-8), David (2 Sam 5:13; 12:11; 19:5), Solomon (1 Kg 10:8; 11:1-4), Rehoboam (2 Chr 11:21), Ahab (1 Kg 20:3-7), and Jehoiachin (2 Kg 24:15). Secondly, in his statement to his wives Lemech acts as a judge, the way a king—and thus a god[20]—would by emitting a verdict of death: "I have slain a man for wounding me, a young man for striking me. If Cain is avenged sevenfold, truly Lemech seventy-sevenfold." (Gen 4:23-24) Notice that in the case of Cain, it is God who is the avenger (v.15). Lemech de facto takes the place of God. By emitting a verdict of death, he commits the ultimate blasphemy of which the kings of Judah and Israel (Ezek 34) were guilty. The two most striking examples of such behavior are David, who took the life of Uriah (2 Sam 11:14-15), and Ahab, who took that of Naboth (1 Kg 21:1-16). So Cain's wish to build a city for protection ends with the rise of kingship that will destroy it. This is the biblical story in a nutshell.

What is important in 1 Timothy, however, is that Lemech's children are split between two wives. His first wife, Adah, bore two sons who are the progenitors of shepherds and troubadours, that is to say, people that are not sedentary, but wander the earth just as Cain was supposed to do. His second wife, Zillah, "bore Tubal-cain; he was the forger (Greek *khalkevs*) of all instruments of bronze and iron." These are two main metals used in gates and bars erected to protect cities and also used to produce instruments of war:

> Thus says the Lord to his anointed, to Cyrus, whose right hand I have grasped, to subdue nations before him and ungird the loins of kings, to open doors before him that gates may not be closed: I will go before you and level the mountains, I will break in pieces the doors of bronze and cut asunder the bars of iron. (Is 45:1-2)

---

[20] Notice the use of "seven" and "seventy seven," reflective of the divine.

And the Lord was with Judah, and he took possession of the hill country, but he could not drive out the inhabitants of the plain, because they had chariots of iron. (Judg 1:19)

Then the people of Israel cried to the Lord for help; for he had nine hundred chariots of iron, and oppressed the people of Israel cruelly for twenty years ... Sisera called out all his chariots, nine hundred chariots of iron, and all the men who were with him, from Harosheth-ha-goiim to the river Kishon. (4:3, 13)

And there came out from the camp of the Philistines a champion named Goliath, of Gath, whose height was six cubits and a span. He had a helmet of bronze on his head, and he was armed with a coat of mail, and the weight of the coat was five thousand shekels of bronze. And he had greaves of bronze upon his legs, and a javelin of bronze slung between his shoulders ... Then Saul clothed David with his armor; he put a helmet of bronze on his head, and clothed him with a coat of mail. (1 Sam 17:4-6, 38)

Since the Hebrew *tubal* is from the same root as *tebel* whose meaning is "the world of human beings,"[21] *tubal-qayin* has the ring of Cain's total human progeny. Consequently, Tubal-Cain, the last in Cain's male progeny, represents the culmination as well as the sum total of that progeny that revolved around the might of the self-sufficient city and its arrogant kingship, both an abhorrence in the eyes of the scriptural God.

The alternative to such human arrogance is offered in the dynasty of Adam-Seth-Enosh (Gen 4:25-26a). The original sounds thus: "And Adam (*'adam*)[22] knew his wife again, and she bore a son and called his name Seth (*šet*), for she said, "God has

---

[21] See *OTI₃* 21-22.

[22] A personal name that functions as the prototype for the human being in general as is evident in its use with the definite article *ha*: "So God created man (*ha'adam*) in his own image, in the image of God he created him; male and female he created them" (Gen 1:27); "then the Lord God formed man (*ha'adam*) of dust from the ground, and breathed into his nostrils the breath of life; and man (*ha'adam*) became a living being." (2:7)

appointed (*šat*)[23] for me another child instead of Abel, for Cain slew him. To Seth (*šet*) also a son was born, and he called his name Enosh (*'enoš*)." Since *'enoš* is the other Hebrew word for human being the sequence *'adam—šet—'enoš* sounds as "a human being posits another human being," which precisely reflects the will of God for humanity[24] (Gen 1:28). This alternative dynasty outlived the one that culminated in the oppressive rule of man over man, for it is neither Cain nor Abel, but Seth (Gen 5:6) and his son Enosh (v.9) who are presented at the head of the progeny of Adam (v.1) which, through Noah (vv.30, 32), remains across the ages down to our own day.

In light of all the above, the names Hymenaeus and Alexander (I Tim 1:20) are to be taken together, rather than as two separate entities. It is inasmuch as the multiplication of the human race ends up with the subjugation of others and the rise of "mighty men of renown" that God is displeased:

> When men began to multiply on the face of the ground, and daughters were born to them, the sons of God saw that the daughters of men were fair; and they took to wife such of them as they chose. Then the Lord said, "My spirit shall not abide in man for ever, for he is flesh, but his days shall be a hundred and twenty years." The Nephilim were on the earth in those days, and also afterward, when the sons of God came in to the daughters of men, and they bore children to them. These were the mighty men that were of old, the men of renown. The Lord saw that the wickedness of man was great in the earth, and that every imagination of the thoughts of his heart was only evil continually. And the Lord was sorry that he had made man on the earth, and it grieved him to his heart. (Gen 6:1-6)

---

[23] Both *šet* and *šat* are from the same Hebrew root *šit* meaning "place, set, appoint."
[24] This is not only his will for man but also for the animal kingdom as well since he said to both: "Be fruitful and multiply." (Gen 1:22, 28)

Similarly, it is to the extent that a Hymenaeus ends up producing the like of Alexander of Macedon that one is dealing with people who are "rejecting conscience" and are "making shipwreck of their faith" (1 Tim 1:19). Thus Hymenaeus and Alexander are presented as prototypes: "By rejecting conscience, certain persons have made shipwreck of their faith, *among them* Hymenaeus and Alexander, whom I have delivered to Satan that they may learn not to blaspheme." (vv.19b-20) The same applies to the pair Hymenaeus and Philetus (2 Tim 2:17) who are also presented as prototypes of wrongdoers: "Avoid such godless chatter, for it will lead people into more and more ungodliness, and their talk will eat its way like gangrene. *Among them* are Hymenaeus and Philetus…" (vv.16-17).

Chapter 2

Vv. 1-7 ¹Παρακαλῶ οὖν πρῶτον πάντων ποιεῖσθαι δεήσεις προσευχὰς ἐντεύξεις εὐχαριστίας ὑπὲρ πάντων ἀνθρώπων, ²ὑπὲρ βασιλέων καὶ πάντων τῶν ἐν ὑπεροχῇ ὄντων, ἵνα ἤρεμον καὶ ἡσύχιον βίον διάγωμεν ἐν πάσῃ εὐσεβείᾳ καὶ σεμνότητι. ³τοῦτο καλὸν καὶ ἀπόδεκτον ἐνώπιον τοῦ σωτῆρος ἡμῶν θεοῦ, ⁴ὃς πάντας ἀνθρώπους θέλει σωθῆναι καὶ εἰς ἐπίγνωσιν ἀληθείας ἐλθεῖν. ⁵εἷς γὰρ θεός, εἷς καὶ μεσίτης θεοῦ καὶ ἀνθρώπων, ἄνθρωπος Χριστὸς Ἰησοῦς, ⁶ὁ δοὺς ἑαυτὸν ἀντίλυτρον ὑπὲρ πάντων, τὸ μαρτύριον καιροῖς ἰδίοις. ⁷εἰς ὃ ἐτέθην ἐγὼ κῆρυξ καὶ ἀπόστολος, ἀλήθειαν λέγω οὐ ψεύδομαι, διδάσκαλος ἐθνῶν ἐν πίστει καὶ ἀληθείᾳ.

> ¹*First of all, then, I urge that supplications, prayers, intercessions, and thanksgivings be made for all men,* ²*for kings and all who are in high positions, that we may lead a quiet and peaceable life, godly and respectful in every way.* ³*This is good, and it is acceptable in the sight of God our Savior,* ⁴*who desires all men to be saved and to come to the knowledge of the truth.* ⁵*For there is one God, and there is one mediator between God and men, the man Christ Jesus,* ⁶*who gave himself as a ransom for all, the testimony to which was borne at the proper time.* ⁷*For this I was appointed a preacher and apostle (I am telling the truth, I am not lying), a teacher of the Gentiles in faith and truth.*

1 Timothy 2:1-7 follows the lead of Romans 13:1-7 by recognizing the functional validity of the Roman imperial and senatorial authority over the expanse of the Roman empire. Hence, Paul requires that prayers be said for those in places of authority, because it is good in the eyes of "God our Savior, who desires all men to be saved and to come to the knowledge of the truth" (1 Tim 2:3b-4), that is, the "truth of the gospel" (Gal 2:5, 14) as preached and taught by Paul to the Gentiles (1 Tim 2:7). An essential element of this gospel teaching is that "there is one

God" (v.5a) in spite of all appearances to the contrary (1 Cor 8:4-6), and the entire world, including that of the Roman authorities, is his. Another essential aspect of the gospel is the absolute lordship of God's emissary over "thrones or dominions or principalities or authorities" (Col 1:16). However, the mission of this "man" Christ Jesus ((1 Tim 2:5; see also Phil 2:6-7) was to "reconcile all things to God, whether on earth or in heaven, making peace by the blood of his cross" (Col 1:20), which is precisely what is stressed here in 1 Timothy 2:5-7.

Vv. 8-15 *⁸Βούλομαι οὖν προσεύχεσθαι τοὺς ἄνδρας ἐν παντὶ τόπῳ ἐπαίροντας ὁσίους χεῖρας χωρὶς ὀργῆς καὶ διαλογισμοῦ. ⁹ Ὡσαύτως [καὶ] γυναῖκας ἐν καταστολῇ κοσμίῳ μετὰ αἰδοῦς καὶ σωφροσύνης κοσμεῖν ἑαυτάς, μὴ ἐν πλέγμασιν καὶ χρυσίῳ ἢ μαργαρίταις ἢ ἱματισμῷ πολυτελεῖ, ¹⁰ἀλλ' ὃ πρέπει γυναιξὶν ἐπαγγελλομέναις θεοσέβειαν, δι' ἔργων ἀγαθῶν. ¹¹Γυνὴ ἐν ἡσυχίᾳ μανθανέτω ἐν πάσῃ ὑποταγῇ· ¹²διδάσκειν δὲ γυναικὶ οὐκ ἐπιτρέπω οὐδὲ αὐθεντεῖν ἀνδρός, ἀλλ' εἶναι ἐν ἡσυχίᾳ. ¹³ Ἀδὰμ γὰρ πρῶτος ἐπλάσθη, εἶτα Εὕα. ¹⁴καὶ Ἀδὰμ οὐκ ἠπατήθη, ἡ δὲ γυνὴ ἐξαπατηθεῖσα ἐν παραβάσει γέγονεν· ¹⁵σωθήσεται δὲ διὰ τῆς τεκνογονίας, ἐὰν μείνωσιν ἐν πίστει καὶ ἀγάπῃ καὶ ἁγιασμῷ μετὰ σωφροσύνης·*

> *⁸I desire then that in every place the men should pray, lifting holy hands without anger or quarreling; ⁹also that women should adorn themselves modestly and sensibly in seemly apparel, not with braided hair or gold or pearls or costly attire ¹⁰but by good deeds, as befits women who profess religion. ¹¹Let a woman learn in silence with all submissiveness. ¹²I permit no woman to teach or to have authority over men; she is to keep silent. ¹³For Adam was formed first, then Eve; ¹⁴and Adam was not deceived, but the woman was deceived and became a transgressor. ¹⁵Yet woman will be saved through bearing children, if she continues in faith and love and holiness, with modesty.*

1 Timothy: Chapter 2

The universality of the "one God" is coextensive with the preaching and teaching that carries him. And, according to Paul, the faith that blossomed out of the seed of the gospel reached "every place" (1 Cor 1:2; 2 Cor 2:14; 1 Thess 1:8):

> We always thank God, the Father of our Lord Jesus Christ, when we pray for you, because we have heard of your faith in Christ Jesus and of the love which you have for all the saints, because of the hope laid up for you in heaven. Of this you have heard before in the word of the truth, the gospel which has come to you, *as indeed in the whole world it is bearing fruit and growing*—so among yourselves, from the day you heard and understood the grace of God in truth. (Col 1:3-6)

That is why Paul's desire is "that in every place the men should pray, lifting holy hands without anger or quarreling." (1 Tim 2:8)

Prayer in the Pauline epistles is essentially a congregational activity that takes place in the *ekklēsia*, the community that is called (*kaleitai*) and comes together (*synerkhomai*) as a gathering or a congregation:

> But in the following instructions I do not commend you, because when you come together (*synerkhesthe*) it is not for the better but for the worse. For, in the first place, when you assemble (*synerkhomenōn*) *as a church* (*en ekklēsia*), I hear that there are divisions among you; and I partly believe it, for there must be factions among you in order that those who are genuine among you may be recognized. When you meet together (*synerkhomenōn*), it is not the Lord's supper that you eat. For in eating, each one goes ahead with his own meal, and one is hungry and another is drunk. What! Do you not have houses to eat and drink in? Or do you despise *the church of God* (*tēs ekklēsias tou Theou*) and humiliate those who have nothing? What shall I say to you? Shall I commend you in this? No, I will not ... So then, my brethren, when you come together to eat, wait for one another—if any one is hungry, let him eat at home—lest you come together (*synerkhēsthe*) to be

condemned. About the other things I will give directions when I come. (1 Cor 11:17-22, 33-34)

It is within this context in 1 Timothy that Paul appeals to the same argument he made in 1 Corinthians (14:33b-36) regarding patrician women speaking in such gatherings as they usually do in their regular "home" gatherings (11:22b). The vocabulary in 1 Timothy and 1 Corinthians clearly correspond:

[I desire] also that women should adorn themselves modestly and sensibly in seemly apparel, not with braided hair or gold or pearls or costly attire but by good deeds, as befits women who profess religion (*theosebeian*). Let a woman *learn* (*manthanetō*) in *silence* (*en hēsykhia*) with all submissiveness (*hypotagē*). I *permit* (*epitrepō*) no woman to teach (*didaskein*) or to have authority over men; she is *to keep silent* (*en hēsykhia*). For Adam was formed first, then Eve; and Adam was not deceived, but the woman *was deceived* (*exapatētheisa*) and became a transgressor. (1 Tim 2:8-14)

As in all the churches of the saints, the women should *keep silence* (*sigatōn*) in the churches. For they are not permitted (*epitrepetai*) to speak, but should be subordinate (*hypotassesthōsan*), as even the law says. If there is anything they desire to know (*mathein*; learn), let them ask their husbands at home. For it is shameful for a woman to speak (*lalein*)[1] in church. What! Did the word of God originate with you, or are you the only ones it has reached? (1 Cor 14:33b-36)

I wish you would bear with me in a little foolishness. Do bear with me! I feel a divine jealousy for you, for I betrothed you to Christ to present you as a pure bride to her one husband. But I am afraid that as the serpent *deceived* (*exēpatēsen*) Eve by his cunning, your thoughts will be led astray from a sincere and pure devotion to Christ. (2 Cor 11:1-3)

---

[1] In the Pauline epistles, the verb *lalein* is usually used with preaching the gospel word and thus corresponds to *didaskein*, "teach" the official teaching (*didaskalia*). Notice how *lalein* is immediately followed by a reference to the "word of God."

1 Timothy: Chapter 2

To understand the verses in 1 Timothy, a detailed discussion of 1 Corinthians 14:33b-36[2] is in order here.

Many scholars consider 1 Corinthians 14:33b-36 to be a later insertion in the original letter since these verses appear to contradict what Paul wrote earlier in 11:5 regarding "any woman who prays or prophesies" (v.4). Paul's instruction in 1 Corinthians 14 is that "the women should keep silence in the churches. For they are not permitted to speak, but should be subordinate, as even the law says. If there is anything they desire to know, let them ask their husbands at home. For it is shameful for a woman to speak in church" (14:34-35). The possibility that 14:33b-36 is a later insertion would be valid only if "the women" in 14:34 and "any woman" of 11:5 were referring to the same subject matter. However, this does not appear to be the case. In chapter 11, woman is compared with man in general and not specifically with her husband.[3] In chapter 14 "the women" are specifically wives since further reference is to "their *own* men (*tous idious andras*)[4] *at home* (*en oikō*)" (v.35). Still, the real difference between the "woman" of chapter 11 and "the women" of chapter 14 is that the former "prophesies" and thus teaches as prophets do (14:31), whereas the latter seek to learn (v.35). Hence, it is incorrect to presume that 14:33b-36 is dealing with the same subject matter as 11:2-16.

To determine what 14:33b-36 is talking about and what dilemma it is trying to solve or at least avoid, we can begin with the three verbs it uses: "*sigatōsan*" (keep silence), "*hypotassesthōsan*" (be subordinate), and "*mathein*" (learn). These were the same verbs just used in conjunction with how the prophets are to behave in the church: "If a revelation is made to another sitting by, let the

---

[2] *C-1Cor* 254-9.
[3] RSV is misleading when in the same verse (11:3) it translates the same original *anēr/andros* once into "man" and once into "her husband."
[4] Which RSV renders correctly as "their husbands."

first be silent (*sigatō*). For you can all prophesy one by one, so that all may learn (*manthanōsin*) and all be encouraged; and the spirits of prophets are subject (*hypotassetai*) to prophets." (vv.30-32) What Paul is driving at is a case of "all the more so." If the prophets, who are granted Paul's preferred spiritual gift, should keep silent to maintain the good order necessary for the membership at large to learn, and if they are to remember that their teaching is subject to the discernment of other prophets, "all the more so" are regular members of the community bound by these rules.

But why does Paul single out the wives to the exclusion of the husbands? Why does he not phrase his instruction in a more encompassing way? Before pursuing this matter, let me point out one more element in vv.33b-36 that brings to mind the second part of chapter 11 that discusses the differentiation between the church (gathering), that is, the function of homes as "house churches" (Rom 16:5; 1 Cor 16:19; Col 4:15; Philem 2), and one's own house (1 Cor 11:21-22). Church gatherings took place in "houses" similar to the homes of the people attending these gatherings, and the "church rules" Paul introduced in 1 Corinthians 11 and 14 sometimes clashed with the common "household rules." When the community gathered together as a church, Paul had to ensure that his church rules, not the household rules, were enforced.

In order to resolve the alleged contradiction between chapters 11 and 14, one should take into account the structure and rules governing a Roman household, which was essentially a hierarchy where everybody, including the wife, was subordinate (*hypotassetai*) to the paterfamilias.[5] Paul hastens to say that this is a matter of Roman as well as scriptural law: "but [women] should be subordinate, as even the law says." (v.34b) This is precisely the

---

[5] See my comments on Col 3:18-4:1 in *C-Col* 87-92.

1 Timothy: Chapter 2   51

centerpiece in Paul's argument since it is surrounded by two parallel statements: "the women should keep silence *in the churches. For they are not permitted to speak,*" (v.34a) and "If there is anything they desire to know, let them ask their husbands at home, *for it is shameful for a woman to speak in church*" (v.35).[6] Church gatherings took place as a *symposion* (table fellowship). In a Roman household, the *symposion* was essentially a social festivity around a common table where socio-political and philosophical ideas were debated. Those usually allowed to speak were the host and the free adult members of the guest households. However, the church gatherings (*ekklēsiai*) instituted by Paul after the manner of the synagogal meetings (*synagōgai*) revolved around scriptural readings followed by exhortatory comments on those readings, which were delivered by the leading members of the gathering. The lack of discussion insured that the Lord's instruction inscribed in scripture be heard unequivocally as well as authoritatively. In the absence of an apostle and in order to maintain the tradition of the *symposion*, Paul allowed more than one person to speak on the condition that those two or three voices be sanctioned by God's spirit (14:27-32). Nonetheless, it was difficult to restrain all free Roman guests from speaking as they were used to doing. Moreover, such stricture would have offended them and might have led to their eventual refusal to attend such meetings. This would have been counterproductive to the dissemination of the gospel word through gatherings held at houses of believing Roman patricians such as Lydia (Acts 16:15),

---

[6] It forms the center of a chiastic structure: [A] As in all the churches of the saints, [B] the women should keep silence in the churches. For they are not permitted to speak, [C] but should be subordinate, as even the law says. [B'] If there is anything they desire to know, let them ask their husbands at home. For it is shameful for a woman to speak in church. [A'] What! Did the word of God originate with you, or are you the only ones it has reached?

Jason (17:5-7), Prisca and Aquila (Rom 16:3-5; 1 Cor 16:19), and Philemon (Philem 1-2).

The head of the Roman household was usually the husband, the paterfamilias, and on rare occasions was the widow until her eldest son became of age or the eldest daughter in an all-female progeny. So, out of deference, Paul's instructions in 1 Corinthians 14:33b-36 allowed a guest paterfamilias to speak—especially that some of the prophets were women—however only to seek learning. Nevertheless, in order not to open the door to a give and take at instructional church gatherings, Paul charged that the guest paterfamilias' wife, who was the second senior member of the family and usually engaged freely in discussions at *symposia*, would refrain from doing so when at a church gathering; any inquiry of or discussion with her husband should be done privately in their own home. Consequently, the text in question is not dealing with "women" in general, but rather with the wives of the guest Roman patricians present at church gatherings.[7] To support his stand Paul uses the same approach that he used in 1 Corinthians 11. In both cases he refers to the unacceptable attitude of women as being *aiskhron* (disgraceful [11:6]; shameful [14:35]). In the first case, however, he appeals to nature (11:14-15), while in the second case he appeals to the (Roman as well as scriptural) law of subordination, which makes his case much more forceful. On the other hand, just as he did in 11:16 in the case of the women prophets, Paul appeals to the tradition of the churches he established and, since the issue is quite sensitive, reference to that tradition is made at the outset (14:33b-34a). Furthermore, to underscore the authority as well as value of this reference to the Pauline tradition, the Apostle ends with the rhetorical question: "What! Did the word of God originate with you, or are you the

---

[7] It does not stand to reason that all women would be targeted in a text just following reference to prophets that could be women. On the other hand, the assumption is that the host wife, being herself a believer (Philem 2; see my comments in *C-Col* 110-11), would have been aware of the rule and would have abstained from speaking.

only ones it has reached?" (v.36) Both statements (vv.33b-34a and v.36) seem to take into consideration the Jewish synagogal tradition,[8] as is the case in 11:2-16. This is intentionally done in order to forego any undue criticism from the Jerusalem church authorities, which criticism could have jeopardized Paul's mission among the Gentiles.[9]

In speaking of the "churches of the saints" (1 Cor 14:33) instead of "the churches of God" (11:16) Paul is clearly referring to the believers and, more specifically, the leaders of the Jerusalem church (16:1-3). In particular Paul is concerned with the acceptance of the offering of the Gentiles that he is to carry to those leaders in Jerusalem. Should those leaders accept that offering, it would confirm their full endorsement of his mission (Rom 15:25-26, 31). Since that offering is the topic of 1 Corinthians 16, it stands to reason that this same concern[10] was on Paul's mind in 1 Corinthians 14.

The last verse (1 Tim 1:15) "Yet woman will be saved through bearing children, if she continues in faith and love and holiness, with modesty," stresses the subject of modesty (*sōphrosynēs*; reasonableness; soundness; good judgment) with which the passage is concerned (v.9),[11] while looking ahead to the many passages that deal with the woman's responsibility for the rearing of the "children" in the church community as both their caretaker and their teacher in the faith (5:2-16).

---

[8] This concern was primary on Paul's mind as is evident in his intentional use of the phrase "the law says (*ho nomos legei*)" (1 Cor 14:34) which brings to mind the Mosaic law over and beyond the Roman law.
[9] See my comments on 1 Cor 11:2-16 in *C-1Cor* 192-200.
[10] This same concern was also expressed in Romans 15.
[11] Actually, in the original the link is ensured through the repetition of the same noun *sōphrosynēs*, which thus functions as an *inclusio* that brackets the entire passage as a literary unit.

Chapter 3

Vv. 1-7 ¹*Πιστὸς ὁ λόγος. Εἴ τις ἐπισκοπῆς ὀρέγεται, καλοῦ ἔργου ἐπιθυμεῖ.* ²*δεῖ οὖν τὸν ἐπίσκοπον ἀνεπίλημπτον εἶναι, μιᾶς γυναικὸς ἄνδρα, νηφάλιον σώφρονα κόσμιον φιλόξενον διδακτικόν,* ³*μὴ πάροινον μὴ πλήκτην, ἀλλὰ ἐπιεικῆ ἄμαχον ἀφιλάργυρον,* ⁴*τοῦ ἰδίου οἴκου καλῶς προϊστάμενον, τέκνα ἔχοντα ἐν ὑποταγῇ, μετὰ πάσης σεμνότητος* ⁵*(εἰ δέ τις τοῦ ἰδίου οἴκου προστῆναι οὐκ οἶδεν, πῶς ἐκκλησίας θεοῦ ἐπιμελήσεται;),* ⁶*μὴ νεόφυτον, ἵνα μὴ τυφωθεὶς εἰς κρίμα ἐμπέσῃ τοῦ διαβόλου.* ⁷*δεῖ δὲ καὶ μαρτυρίαν καλὴν ἔχειν ἀπὸ τῶν ἔξωθεν, ἵνα μὴ εἰς ὀνειδισμὸν ἐμπέσῃ καὶ παγίδα τοῦ διαβόλου.*

> ¹*The saying is sure: If any one aspires to the office of bishop, he desires a noble task.* ²*Now a bishop must be above reproach, the husband of one wife, temperate, sensible, dignified, hospitable, an apt teacher,* ³*no drunkard, not violent but gentle, not quarrelsome, and no lover of money.* ⁴*He must manage his own household well, keeping his children submissive and respectful in every way;* ⁵*for if a man does not know how to manage his own household, how can he care for God's church?* ⁶*He must not be a recent convert, or he may be puffed up with conceit and fall into the condemnation of the devil;* ⁷*moreover he must be well thought of by outsiders, or he may fall into reproach and the snare of the devil.*

Paul is not requiring that the leaders of his churches be "super heroes," given that they are essentially patricians or matriarchs, heads of households (Acts 16:14-16; 17:5-9; 1 Cor 1:11; Philem 1). His general advice to them is the following: "Finally, brethren, whatever is true, whatever is honorable, whatever is just, whatever is pure, whatever is lovely, whatever is gracious, if there is any excellence, if there is anything worthy of praise, think about these things. What you have learned and received and heard and seen in me, do; and the God of peace will be with you" (Phil 4:8-9); "So, whether you eat or drink, or whatever you do, do all to the glory of God. Give no offense to Jews or to Greeks or to the church of God, just as I try to please all men in everything I do, not seeking my own advantage, but that of many, that they may be saved. Be imitators of me, as I am of Christ." (1 Cor 10:31-11:1) By including himself as a model for what he is asking of his hearers, he is indirectly making sure that he is not patronizing them.

So what he asks from the head of a family who would desire to be a bishop is the basics (1 Tim 3:2-3).[1] At the heart of the twelve required qualities—in positions six and seven—he mentions the two that stand at the core of his gospel teaching: be hospitable (*philoxenos*; lover of the stranger)[2] and be apt teacher (*didakton*; knowledgeable, skillful teacher). These qualities will help the bishop to fulfill his duty. His first and foremost task, however, is to manage his household as though it were the household of God (v.5). To do so, he has to have authority over the house "children" the way God has over his. Put otherwise, if his own wife, the mistress of the house, is to be submissive (*en pasē epitagē*; subordinate) to him (2:11), much more so should his children be submissive (*en epitagē*; 3:4). Furthermore, since managing a Roman house, which was essentially a small manor, required "business" experience, the bishop—the paterfamilias in whose home the church of God met—was not to be a "novice" (*neophyton*; v.6), that is to say, either a new convert to the faith or a young paterfamilias such as an heir whose father died prematurely. Finally, since the congregation that gathered in his house would encompass different kinds of people, a paterfamilias

---

[1] For a detailed explanation of the office of bishop, see my comments on Phil 1:1 in *C-Phil* 64-7.
[2] *philoxenia* (care for the stranger) is the other facet of *philadelphia* (brotherly love). See, e.g., Heb 13:1-2: "Let brotherly love (*philadelphia*) continue. Do not neglect to show hospitality to strangers (*philoxenias*), for thereby some have entertained angels unawares."

desiring the office of bishop "must be well thought of by outsiders" (v.7). The seriousness of the last two conditions is reflected in the terminology of the fear that the bishop might "fall to the devil," God's quintessential opponent.

Vv. 8–13 *⁸Διακόνους ὡσαύτως σεμνούς, μὴ διλόγους, μὴ οἴνῳ πολλῷ προσέχοντας, μὴ αἰσχροκερδεῖς, ⁹ἔχοντας τὸ μυστήριον τῆς πίστεως ἐν καθαρᾷ συνειδήσει. ¹⁰καὶ οὗτοι δὲ δοκιμαζέσθωσαν πρῶτον, εἶτα διακονείτωσαν ἀνέγκλητοι ὄντες. ¹¹Γυναῖκας ὡσαύτως σεμνάς, μὴ διαβόλους, νηφαλίους, πιστὰς ἐν πᾶσιν. ¹²διάκονοι ἔστωσαν μιᾶς γυναικὸς ἄνδρες, τέκνων καλῶς προϊστάμενοι καὶ τῶν ἰδίων οἴκων. ¹³οἱ γὰρ καλῶς διακονήσαντες βαθμὸν ἑαυτοῖς καλὸν περιποιοῦνται καὶ πολλὴν παρρησίαν ἐν πίστει τῇ ἐν Χριστῷ Ἰησοῦ.*

> *⁸Deacons likewise must be serious, not double-tongued, not addicted to much wine, not greedy for gain; ⁹they must hold the mystery of the faith with a clear conscience. ¹⁰And let them also be tested first; then if they prove themselves blameless let them serve as deacons. ¹¹The women likewise must be serious, no slanderers, but temperate, faithful in all things. ¹²Let deacons be the husband of one wife, and let them manage their children and their households well; ¹³for those who serve well as deacons gain a good standing for themselves and also great confidence in the faith which is in Christ Jesus.*

The conditions Paul places on those who would become deacons are similar to those of bishops. It would behoove us to digress and explain the function of deacons in the Pauline house churches in order not to read back into the text our contemporary view of the diaconate. Their importance is evident in Philippians where the deacons, along with the bishops, are singled out from among the general brotherhood of the saints: "Paul and Timothy, servants of Christ Jesus, to all the saints in Christ Jesus who are at Philippi, with the bishops and deacons, grace to you and peace from God our Father and the Lord Jesus Christ." (1:1-2)

It is clear from the many instances of the root *diakon*— in the New Testament that it refers to the service a lesser human being offers or gives to someone of higher rank. Thus it is practically equivalent in meaning to the root *doul*— whence comes *doulos* (slave). Can we be more specific as to the difference or at least nuance between the two? A good starting point would be the instances where the root *diakon*— occurs in a setting that is not specifically related to church life. The most "neutral" instance of this, that is to say, when not referring to someone in particular, is found in Jesus' teaching in Luke 17:8:

> Will any one of you, who has a servant (*doulon*) plowing or keeping sheep, say to him when he has come in from the field, 'Come at once and sit down at table'? Will he not rather say to him, 'Prepare supper for me, and gird yourself and serve (*diakonei*) me, till I eat and drink; and afterward you shall eat and drink'? Does he thank the servant (*doulō*) because he did what was commanded? (Lk 17:7-9)

The conclusion is inescapable. Given that the *diakonia* here occurs as a verb qualifying the service of a slave, it is clear that a deacon is none other than a slave *while he is waiting at tables*. Put otherwise, slavery is a state or status; a slave is always a slave. On the other hand, a deacon serving tables is not at all times fulfilling that role. So, the diaconate is functional. This conclusion is corroborated in a Johannine passage where we again find the same general terminology used in conjunction with table fellowship: "Six days before the Passover, Jesus came to Bethany, where Lazarus was, whom Jesus had raised from the dead. There they made him a supper; Martha was serving (*diēkonei*), and Lazarus was one of those at table with him." (Jn 12:1-2)[3]

---

[3] The same applies to the following Lukan passage, parallel to ours, where the justified assumption is that Martha invited Jesus into her house and served him something to eat (which is dutiful in the Middle East): "Now as they went on

This understanding of *diakonia* can be seen in the pericope in Acts where we read about the official institution of the "diaconate" in church life:

> Now in these days when the disciples were increasing in number, the Hellenists murmured against the Hebrews because their widows were neglected in the daily distribution (*diakonia*). And the twelve summoned the body of the disciples and said, "It is not right that we should give up preaching the word of God to serve (*diakonein*) tables. Therefore, brethren, pick out from among you seven men of good repute, full of the Spirit and of wisdom, whom we may appoint to this duty. But we will devote ourselves to prayer and to the ministry (*diakonia*) of the word." (6:1-4).

One finds here a clear instance of the classic weakness of translations in general. The same word *diakonia* is translated differently, giving the impression that the handling of the (gospel) word is of a different nature than that of the daily bread. It is the noun *diakonia*, a specific table fellowship term, that actually defines and qualifies the so-called "ministry" of the word. In other words, the ministry is to be understood against the metaphor of feeding, and not vice versa. Consequently, in order for the divine word to be indeed food for every man (Deut 8:3), it has to be administered at a table gathering. This is precisely what is repeatedly stressed in Acts. Notice how the meal is the matrix of the following passage:

> On the first day of the week, when we were gathered together to break bread, Paul talked with them, intending to depart on the morrow; and he prolonged his speech until midnight. There were

---

their way, he entered a village; and a woman named Martha received him (into her house). And she had a sister called Mary, who sat at the Lord's feet and listened to his teaching. But Martha was distracted with much serving (*diakonian*); and she went to him and said, 'Lord, do you not care that my sister has left me to serve (*diakonein*) alone? Tell her then to help me.'" (Lk 10:38-40)

many lights in the upper chamber where we were gathered. And a young man named Eutychus was sitting in the window. He sank into a deep sleep as Paul talked still longer; and being overcome by sleep, he fell down from the third story and was taken up dead. But Paul went down and bent over him, and embracing him said, "Do not be alarmed, for his life is in him." And when Paul had gone up and had broken bread and eaten, he conversed with them a long while, until daybreak, and so departed. And they took the lad away alive, and were not a little comforted. (20:7-12)

The death and the raising of the young man are totally downplayed and do not interrupt Paul's teaching *while breaking bread* with his listeners.

The centrality of the teaching at table fellowship is found in the Lukan paradigmatic compendium describing the life of the community around the apostolic word:

So those who received his [Peter's] word were baptized, and there were added that day about three thousand souls. And they devoted themselves to the apostles' teaching and fellowship (*koinōnia*), to the breaking of bread and the prayer. And fear came upon every soul; and many wonders and signs were done through the apostles. And all who believed were together (*epi to avto*) and had all things in common (*koina*); and they sold their possessions and goods and distributed them to all, as any had need. And day by day, attending the temple together and breaking bread *in their home*s, they partook of food with glad and generous hearts praising God and having favor with all the people. And the Lord added to their number those who were being saved day by day together with them (*epi to avto*).[4] (Acts 2:41-47)

This focus, if not essential aspect of table fellowship is also found in Paul's statement: "The cup of blessing which we bless, is it not a participation (*koinōnia*) in the blood of Christ? The bread which

---

[4] RSV omits the translation of the last phrase *epi to avto*, which it translated as "together" earlier in v. 44.

we break, is it not a participation (*koinōnia*) in the body of Christ? Because there is one bread, we who are many are one body, for we all partake of the one bread." (1 Cor 10:16-17) What is stressed in the reality of fellowship is the oneness, in the sense of being "at one." However, this oneness is not an intellectual reality articulated in all present reciting the same creed formula. It is the practical oneness expressed in the oneness of table fellowship. This is made clear later in the epistle where Paul threatens the Corinthians with God's ultimate wrath if they do not eat together. The reason being is that the oneness of the table reflects the oneness of the Lord (11:17-34). Thus, duality of tables is not allowed.

All the preceding clearly points back to Galatians 2:1-14, which is the axial passage around which are woven the teachings as well as the narratives of the entire New Testament.[5] There we find precisely that the real test for the fellowship (*koinōnia*) between the Jerusalem pillars, on the one hand, and Paul and Barnabas, on the other hand (Gal 2:9), is not another debate of words, but the actuality of the one table (vv.11-14). It is this kind of crisis at Antioch that precipitated the break between not only Paul and Peter, but even between Paul and his co-apostle Barnabas who was on his side when the *koinōnia* was sealed with the hand-shake!

Yet, here again, as in the case of "bishops and deacons," the greatest danger lies in reading back into the New Testament the practice and understanding of our contemporary Eucharistic gathering. The Lukan passage quoted above (Acts 2:41-47) unequivocally states that the breaking of bread took place "in their homes," indicating that it was a regular meal and not some sort of a "religious" meal at a "religious" place. Notice the difference in Luke's wording between two such gatherings: "And day by day, attending the temple together and breaking bread in their homes

---

[5] See my 4 volumes of *New Testament Introduction: NTI₁, NTI₂, NTI₃, NTI₄*.

(*kat' oikon*; at home)." (v.46) This is only understandable if one recalls that the emerging Pauline "communities" were not yet part of a *religio licita*. Consequently, these home gatherings were not just *ad hoc* informal meals, but factually Pauline "churches" as is clear from the following instances: "Greet Prisca and Aquila, my fellow workers in Christ Jesus ... greet also the church in their house" (Rom 16:3, 5); "The churches of Asia send greetings. Aquila and Prisca, together with the church in their house, send you hearty greetings in the Lord" (1 Cor 16:19); "Give my greetings to the brethren at Laodicea, and to Nympha and the church in her house" (Col 4:15); "To Philemon our beloved fellow worker ... and the church in your house." (Philem 1-2)[6]

Two conclusions are in order. The first is that Paul's frequent use of the root *diakon*— together with that of *doul*— to refer to himself and his co-workers in conjunction with their apostolic activity[7] was not fanciful on his part, but rather intentional. His apostleship, as he wrote in Galatians 2, was continually tested at table fellowship whereby Jews and Gentiles were to be de facto "at one" by sharing the "one" table. The second conclusion is that the diaconate, which is the service of tables without differentiation between Jews and Gentiles or Hebrews and Hellenes (Acts 6:1-5), was an integral part of the church gatherings.

In light of all the preceding, what would one make of 1 Timothy 3:11: "The women likewise must be serious, no slanderers, but temperate, faithful in all things"? Does it refer to deaconesses or deacons' wives or both? The case that this passage refers to deaconesses finds support in Romans 16:1: "I commend to you our sister Phoebe, a deaconess (*diakonon*) of the church at

---

[6] See also Paul's words to the elders of Ephesus: "I did not shrink from declaring to you anything that was profitable, and teaching you in public and from house to house." (Acts 20:20)

[7] Rom 11:13; 15:31; 1 Cor 3:5; 2 Cor 3:3-9; 4:1; 5:18; 6:3, 4; 11:8, 15, 23; Gal 2:17; Eph 3:7; 4:11-12; 6:21; Col 1:7, 23, 25; 4:7; 1 Tim 1:12; 2 Tim 4:5, 11.

Cenchre-ae." The Greek has only one word for the office of the diaconate, *diakonos*, which is a grammatically masculine noun. In English, we have similar instances as in the case of the nouns "professor," "doctor," "president." Paul wanted to make sure that the rules for the diaconate applied "also" (*hōsavtōs*) to the women in this position. The special attention given women deacons is evident in two of the qualifications, "no slanderers" (*mē diabolous*) and "temperate" (*nēphalious*). The latter is a condition that is connected with the bishop (1 Tim 3:2) and not with the deacons. The former is the same word *diabolos* (devil)—used here adjectively, "devilish"—that occurs twice earlier in conjunction with the episcopate (vv.6-7). Had Paul relegated the reference to the women deacons (v. 11) until after v.13, the term "women" could have been taken as referring to the "wives" of the deacons (v.12), which Paul wanted to avoid, since in Greek the same noun *gynē* refers to either a woman or a wife just as the French *femme* or the German *Frau*. Thus, there is no need even to consider the possibility that "women" in v.11 could refer to deacons' wives; otherwise deacons' wives would have been dealt with on par with the bishops! For practical reasons, the office of diaconate may have included couples, but in this case each would have been *diakonos* in one's own right. The mention of "husband of one wife" without the corresponding "wife of one husband," cannot be taken as a counter-argument to this interpretation. The reason is that most languages developed in patriarchal societies and the overwhelming majority of nouns denoting professions or functions are grammatically masculine, which is the case with *diakonos*. The "rule" with such nouns is to take them as applying to both genders. The only striking exception in the entire scripture, Old and New Testaments, is 1 Corinthians 7 that deals with marriage.[8]

Vv. 14-16 ^{14}Ταῦτά σοι γράφω ἐλπίζων ἐλθεῖν πρὸς σὲ ἐν τάχει· ^{15}ἐὰν δὲ βραδύνω, ἵνα εἰδῇς πῶς δεῖ ἐν οἴκῳ θεοῦ

---

[8] See my detailed comments in *C-1Cor* 125-46.

ἀναστρέφεσθαι, ἥτις ἐστὶν ἐκκλησία θεοῦ ζῶντος, στῦλος καὶ ἑδραίωμα τῆς ἀληθείας. ¹⁶καὶ ὁμολογουμένως μέγα ἐστὶν τὸ τῆς εὐσεβείας μυστήριον· ὃς ἐφανερώθη ἐν σαρκί, ἐδικαιώθη ἐν πνεύματι, ὤφθη ἀγγέλοις, ἐκηρύχθη ἐν ἔθνεσιν, ἐπιστεύθη ἐν κόσμῳ, ἀνελήμφθη ἐν δόξῃ.

¹⁴I hope to come to you soon, but I am writing these instructions to you so that, ¹⁵if I am delayed, you may know how one ought to behave in the household of God, which is the church of the living God, the pillar and bulwark of the truth. ¹⁶Great indeed, we confess, is the mystery of our religion: He was manifested in the flesh, vindicated in the Spirit, seen by angels, preached among the nations, believed on in the world, taken up in glory.

At this point Paul uses his characteristic device to explain why he is putting his instructions in writing: his possible delay(s) and the eventuality that he may not come at all (1 Tim 3:14-15a). A classic passage for this is found at the end of the lengthy letter to the Romans:

> This is the reason why I have so often been hindered from coming to you. But now, since I no longer have any room for work in these regions, and since I have longed for many years to come to you, I hope to see you in passing as I go to Spain, and to be sped on my journey there by you, once I have enjoyed your company for a little. At present, however, I am going to Jerusalem with aid for the saints. For Macedonia and Achaia have been pleased to make some contribution for the poor among the saints at Jerusalem; they were pleased to do it, and indeed they are in debt to them, for if the Gentiles have come to share in their spiritual blessings, they ought also to be of service to them in material blessings. When therefore I have completed this, and have delivered to them what has been raised, I shall go on by way of you to Spain; and I know that when I come to you I shall come in the fulness of the blessing of Christ. (15:22-29)

1 Timothy: Chapter 3

In the meantime, in this letter to Timothy lies his legacy as a "deposit" put in the hands of Timothy, the overseer of the "household of God," that is, the church in Ephesus that Paul had built (1 Tim 3:15b; see also 1 Cor 3:10-17 and Eph 2:14-22) upon the "truth" (1 Tim 3:15b) "of the gospel" (Gal 2:5, 14). The studded Pauline terminology of 1 Timothy 3:16 is intentionally done to reflect Paul's teaching inscribed in his letters to the churches:

> Great *indeed, we confess*, (*homologoumenōs*; confessedly) is the mystery of our religion (*evsebeias*): He (*hos*) was manifested in the flesh, vindicated in the Spirit, seen by angels, preached among the nations, believed on in the world, taken up in glory.

The opening adverb *homologoumenōs* (translated as "indeed, we confess"), unique in the New Testament, is from the verb *homologō* (confess, declare openly), which in turn is from the root *logos* (word) and reflects the universal acceptance of the gospel word. The noun *evsebeia* (translated as "religion") has a special resonance in the Greco-Roman ear; it means "piety" (Latin *pietas*) which is the basic religious expression of respect due to all seniors, parents, emperors and governors, and ultimately gods. *evsebeia* is linked with the noun *mystērion* (mystery), something hidden, that is a "secret" known only to a select few. This *mystērion* at some point is to be shared in the open through "revelation" or "manifestation."

The stanza itself is ingeniously constructed. First and foremost, it starts with *hos* (transalted into "He" [RSV]) which is a masculine relative pronoun "who" that does not correspond to *mystērion* (mystery), which is of the neuter grammatical gender.[9] One would have expected the neuter *ho*. Thus Paul was drawing attention to how the mystery was revealed in the *logos* (a masculine noun), that is, the gospel "word" as well as through its carrier, *Iēsous Khristos*

---

[9] Greek, like German, has three grammatical genders: masculine, feminine, and neuter.

(Jesus Christ), which is also grammatically masculine. This allowed Paul to divide the stanza. The first half "was manifested in the flesh, vindicated in (by) the Spirit, seen by (appeared to) angels" follows the movement of Philippians 2:6-11: in spite of his modest appearance, Jesus was vindicated by the power of God and raised into the heavenly sphere. The second half "preached among the nations, believed on in the world, taken up in glory" follows the itinerary of the gospel that spread throughout the world and was acknowledged (*homologoumenōs*) as the divine "word" (Jn 1:1; Rev 5:1).

Chapter 4

Vv. 1-5 ¹Τὸ δὲ πνεῦμα ῥητῶς λέγει ὅτι ἐν ὑστέροις καιροῖς ἀποστήσονταί τινες τῆς πίστεως προσέχοντες πνεύμασιν πλάνοις καὶ διδασκαλίαις δαιμονίων, ²ἐν ὑποκρίσει ψευδολόγων, κεκαυστηριασμένων τὴν ἰδίαν συνείδησιν, ³κωλυόντων γαμεῖν, ἀπέχεσθαι βρωμάτων, ἃ ὁ θεὸς ἔκτισεν εἰς μετάλημψιν μετὰ εὐχαριστίας τοῖς πιστοῖς καὶ ἐπεγνωκόσι τὴν ἀλήθειαν. ⁴ὅτι πᾶν κτίσμα θεοῦ καλὸν καὶ οὐδὲν ἀπόβλητον μετὰ εὐχαριστίας λαμβανόμενον· ⁵ἁγιάζεται γὰρ διὰ λόγου θεοῦ καὶ ἐντεύξεως.

¹Now the Spirit expressly says that in later times some will depart from the faith by giving heed to deceitful spirits and doctrines of demons, ²through the pretensions of liars whose consciences are seared, ³who forbid marriage and enjoin abstinence from foods which God created to be received with thanksgiving by those who believe and know the truth. ⁴For everything created by God is good, and nothing is to be rejected if it is received with thanksgiving; ⁵for then it is consecrated by the word of God and prayer.

As is clear from all the Pauline letters to churches, the congregational gatherings that took place on the first day of the week (1 Cor 16:2) were festive table fellowships. The importance of this Pauline "directive" (v.1) is that the implementation of the gospel, which revolves around the full acceptance of the neighbor, Jew and Gentile alike, is tested at such occasions (Gal 2:11-14). Before their later development into sacramental liturgies, the original Pauline "Lord's suppers" (1 Cor 11:20) were just "agape" meals; however, instead of socio-political or philosophical discussions, the teaching "word of the Lord" (1 Tim 4:5) was delivered for all to hear and then implement in their regular daily lives. As for the food and drink, each would eat whatever one wills without any restrictions on others (Rom 14:1-4; 1Cor 10:25-27; Col 2:16). The specific issue of open table fellowship is evident from the fact that it is the main topic in 1 Tim 4:3-5. The terse two word reference to forbidding marriage at the start of v.3 is thus to be taken in conjunction with what follows, and should be understood as referring to the relationship between a Jew and a Gentile, whether through marriage or at table fellowship. Still, table fellowship takes the lion's share in Paul's comments. This is because marriage is a personal matter, so to speak, whereas table fellowship is a social affair and any misbehavior there is conspicuous and can *openly* affect the gospel itself. This is validated by Paul's comments in Galatians (2:11-14), where he *openly* condemns the behavior of his colleague Peter.

The original 1 Timothy 4:1-5 is filled with terminology that occurs elsewhere in the Pauline corpus in conjunction with the Apostle's harsh invective against his own colleagues who betrayed the gospel. So it makes sense that Timothy, the bishop of the headquarters of the Pauline church, be made aware of the extreme seriousness of this matter. The passage starts with a phrase unique in the New Testament: "Now the Spirit expressly (*rhētōs*) says (*legei*)." In the Pauline corpus, we usually find that the verb "says" (*legei*) has the Lord, the Law, scripture, or a person named in scripture as its subject. In the Pauline corpus, the only other time we hear "the Spirit says" is in Hebrews 3:7, where it is used to introduce a scriptural quotation. Moreover, in 1 Tim 4:1, the verb *legei* is qualified with the adverb *rhētōs*, a unique instance in the entire scripture. This adverb is from the same root as the noun *rhēma* (utterance), usually translated as "word" and its plural *rhēmata* translated into "words." In the original it sounds as though Paul is stressing that what follows are the express words of God's spirit, yet no quotation ensues. Given that the immediate context refers to the Pauline gospel that was "preached among the nations" and "vindicated in the Spirit," it stands to reason to conclude Paul has in mind here the Spirit that speaks through him as *the* Apostle. The vocabulary of the passage (4:1-5) corroborates this since it harks back to Paul's dealings with table fellowship, as

1 Timothy: Chapter 4

well as to his sharp criticism of his opponents. His comments in vv.1-2 recall 2 Corinthians 11 as well as Galatians 2:

> Departing from the faith by giving heed to deceitful (*planois*) spirits and doctrines (*didaskaliais*; teachings) of demons, through the pretensions (*en hypokrisei*) of liars (*psevdologōn*; speaking lies). (1 Tim 4:1-2)

> For if some one comes and preaches another Jesus than the one we preached, or if you receive a different spirit from the one you received, or if you accept a different gospel from the one you accepted, you submit to it readily enough ... For such men are false apostles (*psevdapostoloi*), deceitful (*dolioi*) workmen, disguising themselves as apostles of Christ. And no wonder, for even Satan disguises himself as an angel of light. So it is not strange if his servants also disguise themselves as servants of righteousness. Their end will correspond to their deeds. (2 Cor 11:4, 13-15)

> But because of false brethren (*psevdadelphous*) secretly brought in, who slipped in to spy out our freedom which we have in Christ Jesus, that they might bring us into bondage—to them we did not yield submission even for a moment, that the truth of the gospel might be preserved for you ... For before certain men came from James, he ate with the Gentiles; but when they came he drew back and separated himself, fearing the circumcision party. And with him the rest of the Jews acted insincerely, so that even Barnabas was carried away by their insincerity (*hypokrisei*). But when I saw that they were not straightforward about the truth of the gospel I said to Cephas before them all, "If you, though a Jew, live like a Gentile and not like a Jew, how can you compel the Gentiles to live like Jews. (Gal 2:4-5, 12-14)

The Greek *psevdologōn*, a combination of *psevdos* (lie) and *logōn* (from *logos* [word]), a unique instance in the New Testament, is clearly coined as the antithesis of Paul's "word of truth" (2 Cor

6:7; RSV "truthful speech")[1] as well as "truth of the gospel" (Gal 2:5, 14).[2] The double mention of receiving the food with thanksgiving, once with "knowledge of the truth" (I Tim 4:3), and a second time with the "word of God" (vv. 4-5) is also a reference to table fellowship where "thanksgiving" occurs in conjunction with the gathering of the faithful as one body, when the "word of the Christ" is imparted to them while they "sing psalms and hymns and spiritual songs with thankfulness in your hearts to God":

> And let the peace of Christ rule in your hearts, to which indeed you were called in the one body. And be thankful. Let the word of Christ dwell in you richly, teach and admonish one another in all wisdom, and sing psalms and hymns and spiritual songs with thankfulness in your hearts to God. And whatever you do, in word or deed, do everything in the name of the Lord Jesus, giving thanks to God the Father through him. (Col 3:15-17)[3]

Vv. 6-10 ⁶Ταῦτα ὑποτιθέμενος τοῖς ἀδελφοῖς καλὸς ἔσῃ διάκονος Χριστοῦ Ἰησοῦ, ἐντρεφόμενος τοῖς λόγοις τῆς πίστεως καὶ τῆς καλῆς διδασκαλίας ᾗ παρηκολούθηκας· ⁷τοὺς δὲ βεβήλους καὶ γραώδεις μύθους παραιτοῦ. Γύμναζε δὲ σεαυτὸν πρὸς εὐσέβειαν· ⁸ἡ γὰρ σωματικὴ γυμνασία πρὸς ὀλίγον ἐστὶν ὠφέλιμος, ἡ δὲ εὐσέβεια πρὸς πάντα ὠφέλιμός ἐστιν ἐπαγγελίαν ἔχουσα ζωῆς τῆς νῦν καὶ τῆς μελλούσης. ⁹πιστὸς ὁ λόγος καὶ πάσης ἀποδοχῆς ἄξιος· ¹⁰εἰς τοῦτο γὰρ κοπιῶμεν καὶ ἀγωνιζόμεθα, ὅτι ἠλπίκαμεν ἐπὶ θεῷ ζῶντι, ὅς ἐστιν σωτὴρ πάντων ἀνθρώπων μάλιστα πιστῶν.

---

[1] This is immediately preceded by "genuine love" (*agape anypokritou* [non-hypocritical])" in a series describing Paul's apostolic ministry.
[2] See also Ephesians and Colossians: "In him you also, who have heard the word of truth, the gospel of your salvation" (Eph 1:13); "Of this you have heard before in the word of the truth, the gospel." (Col 1:5)
[3] See also 1 Cor 11:23-24: "For I received from the Lord what I also delivered to you, that the Lord Jesus on the night when he was betrayed took bread, and when he had given thanks, he broke it, and said, 'This is my body which is for you. Do this in remembrance of me.'"

⁶If you put these instructions before the brethren, you will be a good minister of Christ Jesus, nourished on the words of the faith and of the good doctrine which you have followed. ⁷Have nothing to do with godless and silly myths. Train yourself in godliness; ⁸for while bodily training is of some value, godliness is of value in every way, as it holds promise for the present life and also for the life to come. ⁹The saying is sure and worthy of full acceptance. ¹⁰For to this end we toil and strive, because we have our hope set on the living God, who is the Savior of all men, especially of those who believe.

The understanding of the previous passage (1 Tim 4:1-5) within the context of table fellowship finds further evidence in the following verses (6-16): the setting for Paul's directives is the public gathering of the congregation. The table fellowship setting is unequivocal. Timothy is to lay down before (*hypotethemenos* – "put these instructions before") the brethren the "words" of faith and the good doctrine (*didaskalias*; teaching) as a "deacon" (*diakonos*; minister, table server) would. These words Timothy, following the example set by Paul himself as the consummate "deacon" of the gospel, is invited to be "nourished on" (*entrephomenos*) and to "follow" (v.6).

In order to invite Timothy to persevere "till I come" (v.13), Paul uses his classic imagery of the gymnastic arena where one trains (*gymnaze*) continually until one reaches the goal which, in the case of godliness, is "the life to come" (v.8). Paul trained himself in this way while preaching the gospel: "For to this end we toil (*kopiōmen*) and strive (*agōnizometha*) because we have our hope set on the living God." (v.10a) *kopiōmen* is often found in Paul in conjunction with apostolic activity,[4] while *agōnizometha* denotes the *agōn* (stadium race) where one exerts extreme effort to reach

---

[4] 1 Cor 4:12; 15:10; 16:16; Gal 4:11; Eph 4:28; Phil 2:16; Col 1:29.

the finish line.[5] Timothy has to persevere in that teaching because, although "the living God is the Savior of all men," one can only hope for that salvation since it is granted to those who remain trustworthy. The translation of this text does not reflect the word play of the original where the adjective *pistos* brackets the statement in vv.9-10: "*Pistos ho logos* (Trustworthy is the [gospel] word) and worthy of full acceptance. For to this end we toil and strive, because we have our hope set on the living God, who is the Savior of all men, more specifically of those who (remain) *pistōn* (trustworthy, trusting [in the gospel word])." Matthew captured this imagery of perseverance until the end and linked it to the coming judgment by the Son of Man:

> Behold, I send you out as sheep in the midst of wolves; so be wise as serpents and innocent as doves. Beware of men; for they will deliver you up to councils, and flog you in their synagogues, and you will be dragged before governors and kings for my sake, to bear testimony before them and the Gentiles. When they deliver you up, do not be anxious how you are to speak or what you are to say; for what you are to say will be given to you in that hour; for it is not you who speak, but the Spirit of your Father speaking through you. Brother will deliver up brother to death, and the father his child, and children will rise against parents and have them put to death; and you will be hated by all for my name's sake. *But he who endures to the end will be saved.* When they persecute you in one town, flee to the next; for truly, I say to you, you will not have gone through all the towns of Israel, before the Son of man comes. (Mt 10:16-23)

> Then they will deliver you up to tribulation, and put you to death; and you will be hated by all nations for my name's sake. And then many will fall away, and betray one another, and hate one

---

[5] Hence the English "agony" and "agonize." See Phil 1:30; Col 2:1; 1 Thess 2:2 for the noun *agōn*; 1 Cor 9:25; Col 1:29; 4:12 (where it is translated as "remembering earnestly") for the verb *agōnizomai*; and 1 Tim 6:12 (Fight the good fight of the faith); 2 Tim 4:7 (I have fought the good fight, I have finished the race, I have kept the faith) for both ther moun and the verb.

another. And many false prophets will arise and lead many astray. And because wickedness is multiplied, most men's love will grow cold. *But he who endures to the end will be saved.* And this gospel of the kingdom will be preached throughout the whole world, as a testimony to all nations; and then the end will come … And if those days had not been shortened, no human being would be saved; but for the sake of the elect those days will be shortened … For as the lightning comes from the east and shines as far as the west, so will be the coming of the Son of man. (24:9-13, 22, 27)

When the Son of man comes in his glory, and all the angels with him, then he will sit on his glorious throne. Before him will be gathered all the nations, and he will separate them one from another as a shepherd separates the sheep from the goats, and he will place the sheep at his right hand, but the goats at the left. (25:31-33)

Vv. 11-16 ¹¹Παράγγελλε ταῦτα καὶ δίδασκε. ¹²Μηδείς σου τῆς νεότητος καταφρονείτω, ἀλλὰ τύπος γίνου τῶν πιστῶν ἐν λόγῳ, ἐν ἀναστροφῇ, ἐν ἀγάπῃ, ἐν πίστει, ἐν ἁγνείᾳ. ¹³ἕως ἔρχομαι πρόσεχε τῇ ἀναγνώσει, τῇ παρακλήσει, τῇ διδασκαλίᾳ. ¹⁴μὴ ἀμέλει τοῦ ἐν σοὶ χαρίσματος, ὃ ἐδόθη σοι διὰ προφητείας μετὰ ἐπιθέσεως τῶν χειρῶν τοῦ πρεσβυτερίου. ¹⁵ταῦτα μελέτα, ἐν τούτοις ἴσθι, ἵνα σου ἡ προκοπὴ φανερὰ ᾖ πᾶσιν. ¹⁶ἔπεχε σεαυτῷ καὶ τῇ διδασκαλίᾳ, ἐπίμενε αὐτοῖς· τοῦτο γὰρ ποιῶν καὶ σεαυτὸν σώσεις καὶ τοὺς ἀκούοντάς σου.

¹¹Command and teach these things. ¹²Let no one despise your youth, but set the believers an example in speech and conduct, in love, in faith, in purity. ¹³Till I come, attend to the public reading of scripture, to preaching, to teaching. ¹⁴Do not neglect the gift you have, which was given you by prophetic utterance when the council of elders laid their hands upon you. ¹⁵Practice these duties, devote yourself to them, so that all may see your progress. ¹⁶Take heed to yourself and to your teaching; hold to that, for by so doing you will save both yourself and your hearers.

This compact passage is one the most impressive in scripture. First and foremost, the "good doctrine (*didaskalia*; teaching)" on which Timothy was nourished and bred (1 Tim 4:6) brackets the passage as *inclusio*: "Command and teach (*didaske*) these things ... Take heed to yourself and to your teaching (*didaskalias*); hold to that, for by so doing you will save both yourself and your hearers." (vv.11, 16a) The reason is given in no uncertain terms: not only his hearers' salvation, but also his own salvation depends on it. That is why he is to "continue (KJV), persevere (JB)" (*epimene*) in this activity. RSV's "hold to" weakens the original intent, since it could be perceived as referring to the content of the teaching rather than its delivery to the community. Paul's intention is to invite Timothy to follow the path of Moses and Jeremiah: the message holds priority over the person who may well—and actually did—prove wanting. That Paul had those two prophets in mind is betrayed in the mention of Timothy's "young age" (*neotētos*; v.12). Moses was younger than his brother Aaron, and Jeremiah's excuse to the Lord was that he was "only a youth (*neōteros*)" (Jer 1:6). Thus, Timothy's "young age" should not be considered an impediment to his authority (1 Tim 4:12a) since such authority was secured through his appointment by the empowering laying on of the hands[6] of the council of "elders" and, beyond them, "by prophetic utterance" that ultimately proceeds from God (v.14). Since Timothy is appointed through "prophecy" just as the "prophets" Moses and Jeremiah were, he "sits on Moses' seat" (Mt 23:2). Furthermore, Timothy is to command and teach (*didaske*) the "good doctrine (*didaskalias*; teaching)" (1 Tim 4:11) "until I come" (v.13), that is to say, indefinitely, since Paul may not come at all:

> For I am already on the point of being sacrificed; the time of my departure has come. I have fought the good fight, I have finished the race, I have kept the faith. Henceforth there is laid up for me

---

[6] Hand is tantamount to power in scripture.

the crown of righteousness, which the Lord, the righteous judge, will award to me on that Day, and not only to me but also to all who have loved his appearing. (2 Tim 4:6-8)

For an ear attentive of scripture Paul is in fact encouraging Timothy to follow in his footsteps: "Practice these duties, devote yourself to them, so that your progress (*prokopē*) may be manifest (*phanera*)."[7] (1 Tim 4:15). The noun *prokopē* occurs in the New Testament only twice more and in the same context:

> I want you to know, brethren, that what has happened to me has really served to advance (*eis prokopēn*; unto the advancement [progress] of) the gospel, so that it has become known (*phanerous*; manifest) throughout the whole praetorian guard and to all the rest that my imprisonment is for Christ; and most of the brethren have been made confident in the Lord because of my imprisonment, and are much more bold to speak the word of God without fear ... For I know that through your prayers and the help of the Spirit of Jesus Christ this will turn out for my deliverance, as it is my eager expectation and hope that I shall not be at all ashamed, but that with full courage now as always Christ will be honored in my body, whether by life or by death. For to me to live is Christ, and to die is gain. If it is to be life in the flesh, that means fruitful labor for me. Yet which I shall choose I cannot tell. I am hard pressed between the two. My desire is to depart and be with Christ, for that is far better. But to remain in the flesh is more necessary on your account. Convinced of this, I know that I shall remain and continue with you all, for your progress (*prokopēn*) and joy in the faith, so that in me you may have ample cause to glory in Christ Jesus, because of my coming to you again. (Phil 1:12-14; 19-25)

Paul's own "progress" on the gospel's way would not lead to the "progress" of his flock in Philippi unless he relegates his own desires and preferences to the backburner and gives all his attention to their "needs." This is nothing other than

---

[7] I am following JB that is closer to the original than KJV (may appear) and RSV (that all may see [your progress]).

implementing in his own life the heart of the gospel that he is serving: love for the needy neighbor. That is why, at the center of the fivefold command to Timothy[8] to lead an "exemplary" life lies that love: "Let no one despise your youth, but set the believers an example in speech and conduct, in love, in faith, in purity." (1 Tim 4:12) Such is no wonder since his preaching and teaching are to ensue from the scriptural reading and not from his own mind: "Till I come, attend to the public reading of scripture, to preaching, to teaching." (v.13) As Paul twice wrote, the entire Law is summed up in the commandment of love:

> Owe no one anything, except to love one another; for he who loves his neighbor has fulfilled the law. The commandments, "You shall not commit adultery, You shall not kill, You shall not steal, You shall not covet," and any other commandment, are summed up in this sentence, "You shall love your neighbor as yourself." Love does no wrong to a neighbor; therefore love is the fulfilling of the law. (Rom 13:8-10)

> For the whole law is fulfilled in one word, "You shall love your neighbor as yourself." (Gal. 5:14)

---

[8] Reminiscent of the five books of the Law.

Chapter 5

5:1-6:1 ¹Πρεσβυτέρῳ μὴ ἐπιπλήξῃς ἀλλὰ παρακάλει ὡς πατέρα, νεωτέρους ὡς ἀδελφούς, ²πρεσβυτέρας ὡς μητέρας, νεωτέρας ὡς ἀδελφὰς ἐν πάσῃ ἁγνείᾳ. ³Χήρας τίμα τὰς ὄντως χήρας. ⁴εἰ δέ τις χήρα τέκνα ἢ ἔκγονα ἔχει, μανθανέτωσαν πρῶτον τὸν ἴδιον οἶκον εὐσεβεῖν καὶ ἀμοιβὰς ἀποδιδόναι τοῖς προγόνοις· τοῦτο γάρ ἐστιν ἀπόδεκτον ἐνώπιον τοῦ θεοῦ. ⁵ἡ δὲ ὄντως χήρα καὶ μεμονωμένη ἤλπικεν ἐπὶ θεὸν καὶ προσμένει ταῖς δεήσεσιν καὶ ταῖς προσευχαῖς νυκτὸς καὶ ἡμέρας, ⁶ἡ δὲ σπαταλῶσα ζῶσα τέθνηκεν. ⁷καὶ ταῦτα παράγγελλε, ἵνα ἀνεπίλημπτοι ὦσιν. ⁸εἰ δέ τις τῶν ἰδίων καὶ μάλιστα οἰκείων οὐ προνοεῖ, τὴν πίστιν ἤρνηται καὶ ἔστιν ἀπίστου χείρων. ⁹Χήρα καταλεγέσθω μὴ ἔλαττον ἐτῶν ἑξήκοντα γεγονυῖα, ἑνὸς ἀνδρὸς γυνή, ¹⁰ἐν ἔργοις καλοῖς μαρτυρουμένη, εἰ ἐτεκνοτρόφησεν, εἰ ἐξενοδόχησεν, εἰ ἁγίων πόδας ἔνιψεν, εἰ θλιβομένοις ἐπήρκεσεν, εἰ παντὶ ἔργῳ ἀγαθῷ ἐπηκολούθησεν. ¹¹νεωτέρας δὲ χήρας παραιτοῦ· ὅταν γὰρ καταστρηνιάσωσιν τοῦ Χριστοῦ, γαμεῖν θέλουσιν ¹²ἔχουσαι κρίμα ὅτι τὴν πρώτην πίστιν ἠθέτησαν· ¹³ἅμα δὲ καὶ ἀργαὶ μανθάνουσιν περιερχόμεναι τὰς οἰκίας, οὐ μόνον δὲ ἀργαὶ ἀλλὰ καὶ φλύαροι καὶ περίεργοι, λαλοῦσαι τὰ μὴ δέοντα ¹⁴Βούλομαι οὖν νεωτέρας γαμεῖν, τεκνογονεῖν, οἰκοδεσποτεῖν, μηδεμίαν ἀφορμὴν διδόναι τῷ ἀντικειμένῳ λοιδορίας χάριν· ¹⁵ἤδη γάρ τινες ἐξετράπησαν ὀπίσω τοῦ σατανᾶ. ¹⁶εἴ τις πιστὴ ἔχει χήρας, ἐπαρκείτω αὐταῖς καὶ μὴ βαρείσθω ἡ ἐκκλησία, ἵνα ταῖς ὄντως χήραις ἐπαρκέσῃ. ¹⁷Οἱ καλῶς προεστῶτες πρεσβύτεροι διπλῆς τιμῆς ἀξιούσθωσαν, μάλιστα οἱ κοπιῶντες ἐν λόγῳ καὶ διδασκαλίᾳ. ¹⁸λέγει γὰρ ἡ γραφή· βοῦν ἀλοῶντα οὐ φιμώσεις, καί· ἄξιος ὁ ἐργάτης τοῦ μισθοῦ αὐτοῦ. ¹⁹κατὰ πρεσβυτέρου κατηγορίαν μὴ παραδέχου, ἐκτὸς εἰ μὴ ἐπὶ δύο ἢ τριῶν μαρτύρων. ²⁰Τοὺς ἁμαρτάνοντας ἐνώπιον πάντων ἔλεγχε, ἵνα καὶ οἱ λοιποὶ φόβον ἔχωσιν. ²¹Διαμαρτύρομαι ἐνώπιον τοῦ θεοῦ καὶ Χριστοῦ Ἰησοῦ καὶ τῶν ἐκλεκτῶν ἀγγέλων, ἵνα ταῦτα φυλάξῃς χωρὶς προκρίματος, μηδὲν ποιῶν κατὰ πρόσκλισιν. ²²χεῖρας ταχέως μηδενὶ ἐπιτίθει μηδὲ κοινώνει ἁμαρτίαις ἀλλοτρίαις· σεαυτὸν ἁγνὸν τήρει. ²³Μηκέτι ὑδροπότει, ἀλλὰ οἴνῳ ὀλίγῳ χρῶ διὰ τὸν στόμαχον καὶ τὰς πυκνάς σου ἀσθενείας. ²⁴Τινῶν ἀνθρώπων αἱ ἁμαρτίαι πρόδηλοί εἰσιν προάγουσαι εἰς κρίσιν, τισὶν δὲ καὶ ἐπακολουθοῦσιν· ²⁵ὡσαύτως καὶ τὰ ἔργα τὰ καλὰ πρόδηλα, καὶ τὰ ἄλλως ἔχοντα κρυβῆναι οὐ δύνανται.

6:1 Ὅσοι εἰσὶν ὑπὸ ζυγὸν δοῦλοι, τοὺς ἰδίους δεσπότας πάσης τιμῆς ἀξίους ἡγείσθωσαν, ἵνα μὴ τὸ ὄνομα τοῦ θεοῦ καὶ ἡ διδασκαλία βλασφημῆται. ²οἱ δὲ πιστοὺς ἔχοντες δεσπότας μὴ καταφρονείτωσαν, ὅτι ἀδελφοί εἰσιν, ἀλλὰ μᾶλλον δουλευέτωσαν, ὅτι πιστοί εἰσιν καὶ ἀγαπητοὶ οἱ τῆς εὐεργεσίας ἀντιλαμβανόμενοι. Ταῦτα δίδασκε καὶ παρακάλει.

> ¹*Do not rebuke an older man but exhort him as you would a father; treat younger men like brothers,* ²*older women like mothers, younger women like sisters, in all purity.* ³*Honor widows who are real widows.* ⁴*If a widow has children or grandchildren, let them first learn their religious duty to their own family and make some return to their parents; for this is acceptable in the sight of God.* ⁵*She who is a real widow, and is left all alone, has set her hope on God and continues in supplications and prayers night and day;* ⁶*whereas she who is self-indulgent is dead even while she lives.* ⁷*Command this, so that they may be without reproach.* ⁸*If any one does not provide for his relatives, and especially for his own family, he has disowned the faith and is worse than an unbeliever.* ⁹*Let a widow be enrolled if she is not less than sixty years of age, having been the wife of one husband;* ¹⁰*and she must be well attested for her good deeds, as one who has brought up children, shown hospitality, washed the feet of the saints, relieved the afflicted, and devoted herself to doing good in every way.* ¹¹*But refuse to enrol younger widows; for when they grow wanton against Christ they desire to marry,* ¹²*and so they incur condemnation for having violated their first pledge.* ¹³*Besides that, they learn to be idlers, gadding about from house to house, and not only idlers but gossips and busybodies, saying what they should not.* ¹⁴*So I would have younger widows*

*marry, bear children, rule their households, and give the enemy no occasion to revile us. ¹⁵For some have already strayed after Satan. ¹⁶If any believing woman*ᵉ *has relatives who are widows, let her assist them; let the church not be burdened, so that it may assist those who are real widows. ¹⁷Let the elders who rule well be considered worthy of double honor, especially those who labor in preaching and teaching; ¹⁸for the scripture says, "You shall not muzzle an ox when it is treading out the grain," and, "The laborer deserves his wages." ¹⁹Never admit any charge against an elder except on the evidence of two or three witnesses. ²⁰As for those who persist in sin, rebuke them in the presence of all, so that the rest may stand in fear. ²¹In the presence of God and of Christ Jesus and of the elect angels I charge you to keep these rules without favor, doing nothing from partiality. ²²Do not be hasty in the laying on of hands, nor participate in another man's sins; keep yourself pure. ²³No longer drink only water, but use a little wine for the sake of your stomach and your frequent ailments. ²⁴The sins of some men are conspicuous, pointing to judgment, but the sins of others appear later. ²⁵So also good deeds are conspicuous; and even when they are not, they cannot remain hidden.*

⁶:¹Let all who are under the yoke of slavery regard their masters as worthy of all honor, so that the name of God and the teaching may not be defamed. ²Those who have believing masters must not be disrespectful on the ground that they are brethren; rather they must serve all the better since those who benefit by their service are believers and beloved. Teach and urge these duties.

In chapter 5 Paul turns to the general "house rules" regarding the young and the old (1 Tim 5:1-2). It is the elders, however, who are his main concern (vv.3-20), and in this category it is the widows who get the lion's share (vv.3-16). Among these he singles out the "real" (*ontōs*; indeed) widows whom Timothy must "honor." To assess the special value of this injunction one is to hear it within the context of the entire letter where honor is due exclusively to seniors. First and foremost all must honor God (1:17; 6:16). This reminder brackets as *inclusio* the entire letter. It is as though anything and everything that takes place in the Pauline house churches is to take place under the aegis of the absolute paterfamilias: "For this reason I bow my knees before the Father (*patera*), from whom every family (*patria*; from the same root as *patera*) in heaven and on earth is named." (Eph 3:14-15)[1] In the Roman empire every paterfamilias would be due a similar honor (1 Tim 6:1). The reason given here is so that the teaching would not be defamed (1 Tim 6:1). This in turn explains the command in 5:17 that the "elders who rule well be considered worthy of double honor, especially those who labor in preaching and teaching (*didaskalia*)." One can, therefore, imagine how powerful this must have sounded given that the initial injunction to honor a human being had widows in mind! And, as if this was not enough, let us try to imagine how the entire matter sounded to a Greek ear. Timothy, *the* teaching elder, whose name in Greek *Timotheos* means either "the one who honors God" or "the one whom God honors," is himself commanded by Paul to "honor (*tima*) widows who are real widows" (5:3). The only other instances of *tima* (imperative second person singular of the verb *timān*) in the New Testament are all part of the Decalogue commandment "Honor your father and your mother" (Mt 15:4; 19:9; Mk 7:10: 10:19; Jn 5:23; Eph 6:2). Consequently, honoring the widows is equal in value as honoring one's mother as Paul himself just underscored (1 Tim 5:1-2)

The strictness of the passage about the widows (vv.3-16) is most impressive. In Paul's time, life expectancy was much shorter than it is today, so the condition that she be "not less than sixty years of age" (v.9) to be considered "indeed" (*ontōs*) a widow meant that not too many women fit into that category. This already short list

---

[1] The Greek *patria* has a wide range of meanings from a clan or a tribe, to an entire nation. The French *patrie* is the counterpart of the English "nation."

was to be tightly overseen since Paul required Timothy to "command" (v.7) that such widows be "catalogued" (*katalegesthō*; enrolled), the unique instance of that verb in the New Testament.[2] Even more, the one hoping to be catalogued to receive special aid has to have shown during her lifetime that she took care of others when she was in a position to do so (v.10), and that she had been married only once (v.9), meaning that she did not tried to find refuge through a second marriage. Furthermore, if she has children or grandchildren of her own who can accommodate her needs, then she should not burden the congregation (v.4): "She who is a real widow, and is *left all alone* (*memonōmenē*),[3] has set her hope on God and continues in supplications and prayers night and day; whereas she who is self-indulgent is dead even while she lives." (vv.5-6) As for the younger widows, let them "remarry" (v.11) in order to "bear children"[4] and "rule a household" (*oikodespotein*; v.14) by "bringing up their children" as the real widows have done (v.10). Hopefully, in this way, the children and grandchildren of the widows will take care of them (v.4). Paul is strictly prohibiting the congregation from supporting those who are not identified as "real" widows (v.16), and even labels such a practice as the work of Satan (v.15).

Given that the only other instance in the Pauline corpus where we hear of widows is 1 Corinthians 7, it stands to reason to consider that Paul is expanding on this subject in his directives to Timothy concerning the house church in Ephesus (1 Tim 5:16). The connection with 1 Corinthians is evident. In the next passage (1 Tim 5:17-23) one finds a scriptural quotation (Deut 25:4) that occurs exclusively in these two letters: "You shall not muzzle an ox when it is treading out the grain." (1 Cor 9:9; 1 Tim 5:18) To be sure, in the first case, the intended is the apostle; in the second

---

[2] Behind "refuse to enroll" (v.11) lies the Greek *paraitou* whose meaning is "reject, refuse."
[3] This is the unique instance of *memonōmenē* in the New Testament.
[4] See earlier 2:15.

case, the Mosaic rule is applied to the elders commissioned to teach. The closeness in thought is betrayed in that the elders are portrayed in "apostolic" terminology: "Let the elders who rule well be considered worthy of double honor, especially those who labor (*kopiōntes*) in preaching (*logō*; word) and teaching (*didaskalia*)." (v.17) By using the combination of "labor" and "word" in conjunction with the "teaching," Paul is underscoring that, just as the bishop is to uphold the apostolic teaching that was given to him as a deposit and is not to tampered with it, that same rule applies to the elders who share that duty: they are to teach while "sitting in the chair of the Apostle." With such worthiness, however, comes greater responsibility in that the sins of the elders are to be dealt with publicly, not only before the others (v.20), but also before the divine council and, consequently, without favor or partiality (v.21).[5] That is why Timothy should be careful "not to be hasty in the laying on of hands" on such elders (v.22a).

The second part of v.22 and the entire v.23 present a conundrum. Since the preceding reference is to "sin" committed by teaching elders (v.20a), does the prohibition to "participate in someone's sin" (v.22b) also describe the sin of an elder? The conjunction "nor" linking v.22b to v.22a points in that direction. Timothy is obviously the main agent in the laying on of hands (v.22a), but how should one understand his participation in the sin of an elder he ordains? What is the meaning of "keep yourself pure (*hagnon*)" (v.22c) in that context? Is it purity from sin? And, if so, what does Paul's dietary suggestion regarding drinking "not only water" but also "a little wine" (v.23) have to do with all the preceding? I am convinced the solution will be found if one understands v. 23 against the background of the story we hear at the beginning of the Book of Daniel:

---

[5] Concerning the angels being part of the divine council, see my comments on 1 Cor 11:10 in *C-1Cor* 200.

In the third year of the reign of Jehoiakim king of Judah, Nebuchadnezzar king of Babylon came to Jerusalem and besieged it. And the Lord gave Jehoiakim king of Judah into his hand, with some of the vessels of the house of God; and he brought them to the land of Shinar, to the house of his god, and placed the vessels in the treasury of his god. Then the king commanded Ashpenaz, his chief eunuch, to bring some of the people of Israel, both of the royal family and of the nobility, youths without blemish, handsome and skilful in all wisdom, endowed with knowledge, understanding learning, and competent to serve in the king's palace, and to teach them the letters and language of the Chaldeans. The king assigned them a daily portion of the rich food which the king ate, and of the wine which he drank. They were to be educated for three years, and at the end of that time they were to stand before the king. Among these were Daniel, Hananiah, Misha-el, and Azariah of the tribe of Judah. And the chief of the eunuchs gave them names: Daniel he called Belteshazzar, Hananiah he called Shadrach, Misha-el he called Meshach, and Azariah he called Abednego. But Daniel resolved that he would not defile himself with the king's rich food, or with the wine which he drank; therefore he asked the chief of the eunuchs to allow him not to defile himself. And God gave Daniel favor and compassion in the sight of the chief of the eunuchs; and the chief of the eunuchs said to Daniel, "I fear lest my lord the king, who appointed your food and your drink, should see that you were in poorer condition than the youths who are of your own age. So you would endanger my head with the king." Then Daniel said to the steward whom the chief of the eunuchs had appointed over Daniel, Hananiah, Misha-el, and Azariah, "Test your servants for ten days; let us be given vegetables to eat and water to drink. Then let our appearance and the appearance of the youths who eat the king's rich food be observed by you, and according to what you see deal with your servants." So he hearkened to them in this matter, and tested them for ten days. At the end of ten days it was seen that they were better in appearance and fatter in flesh than all the youths who ate the king's rich food. So the steward took away their rich food and the wine they were to drink, and gave them vegetables. (1:1-16)

Since, as is clear from this passage, wine was usually imbibed at rich table spreads, Paul's "suggestion" is actually an oblique "order" never to renege on common table fellowship, which is in line with the teaching concerning the validity of all food and drink when ingested with thanksgiving (1 Tim 4:3-4). So the purity (*hagnon*) required from Timothy (5:22c) is one of conduct— [treat] younger women like sisters, in all purity (*hagneia*; v.2b)— and, moreover, as a bishop he should teach it: "Command and teach these things. Let no one despise your youth, but set the believers an example in speech and *conduct*, in love, in faith, in purity (*hagneia*)." (4:11-12)[6] In this particular case, the conduct is one practiced at common meals as is evident in Paul's use of *koinōnei* (participate; 5:22b), from the same root as *koinōnia*, which specifically connotes table fellowship.[7] So in 5:22-23, Paul is asking Timothy to make sure that he would not ordain any elder who does not endorse the common table fellowship, "with thanksgiving," between Jews and Gentiles (4:3-4). His and their final judgment, when everything, including the hidden things, shall be revealed, hangs on that (5:24-25).

At this point, I should like to revisit v.18: "for the scripture says, 'You shall not muzzle an ox when it is treading out the grain,' and, 'The laborer deserves his wages.'" This is the only instance in the entire New Testament where we have a quotation from the New Testament itself *as scripture*: "The laborer deserves his wages" (Lk 10:7).[8] In my discussion of Colossians 4:10-17, I have argued that that passage was not only canonizing the Pauline corpus but actually the Gospels of at least Mark and Luke.[9] 2 Peter takes us a step further in scripturalizing Paul's letters by placing them on par with the Old Testament: "So also our beloved brother Paul wrote

---

[6] These, together with *hagnon* (pure) in 5:22c, are the only instances of the root *hagn*— in the letter.
[7] See my comments especially in *C-1Cor* 180-4.
[8] The parallel statement in Mt 10:10 is "The laborer deserves his food."
[9] *C-Col* 102-3.

to you according to the wisdom given him, speaking of this as he does in all his letters. There are some things in them hard to understand, which the ignorant and unstable twist to their own destruction, as they do the other scriptures." (3:15b-16) 1 Timothy takes the last step by scripturalizing the canonical Gospels. All this militates for the thesis defended in my entire body of work on the New Testament, that that entire literature is a closely knit product of the one (Pauline) school, just as I have argued in my work on the Old Testament books that they too are the product of the one (Ezekelian) school.

Paul ends his house rules with his instruction to the slaves (6:1-2). Singling them out here corresponds to what we hear in Colossians and Ephesians. After the lengthy digression on husbands and wives in Ephesians (5:22-33), which is covered in only two verses in Colossians (3:18-19), Paul summarizes his instruction to the slaves (Eph 6:5-8; Col 3:22-25). The reason for such instruction is explained in Corinthians and in Romans:

> Every one should remain in the state in which he was called. Were you a slave when called? Never mind. But if you can gain your freedom, avail yourself of the opportunity. For he who was called in the Lord as a slave is a freedman of the Lord. Likewise he who was free when called is a slave of Christ. You were bought with a price; do not become slaves of men. So, brethren, in whatever state each was called, there let him remain with God. (1 Cor 7:20-24)

> But now that you have been set free from sin and have become slaves of God, the return you get is sanctification and its end, eternal life … For the law of the Spirit of life in Christ Jesus has set me free from the law of sin and death. (Rom 6:22; 8:2)

In 1 Timothy an additional reason is set forth. In case of believing masters, robbing them of the care that a slave would provide to them is showing lack of love for a believing "brother" (6:2a). What is still worse is that in such case the "teaching" (*didaskalia*), which Timothy is in charge of (4:6), and even God's name will "be defamed (*blasphēmētai*; blasphemed)" (6:1b); furthermore, the perpetrators will have to be "delivered to Satan that they may learn not to blaspheme (*blasphēmein*)" (1:20b). Timothy is to "teach (*didaske*) and urge (*parakalei*; exhort) these duties (*tavta*; these things)" (6:2b) as a bishop is supposed to do: "Command (*parangelle*) and teach (*didaske*) these things (*tavta*)" (4:11).

Chapter 6

Vv. 3-21 ³ εἴ τις ἑτεροδιδασκαλεῖ καὶ μὴ προσέρχεται ὑγιαίνουσιν λόγοις τοῖς τοῦ κυρίου ἡμῶν Ἰησοῦ Χριστοῦ καὶ τῇ κατ᾽ εὐσέβειαν διδασκαλίᾳ, ⁴ τετύφωται, μηδὲν ἐπιστάμενος, ἀλλὰ νοσῶν περὶ ζητήσεις καὶ λογομαχίας, ἐξ ὧν γίνεται φθόνος ἔρις βλασφημίαι, ὑπόνοιαι πονηραί, ⁵ διαπαρατριβαὶ διεφθαρμένων ἀνθρώπων τὸν νοῦν καὶ ἀπεστερημένων τῆς ἀληθείας, νομιζόντων πορισμὸν εἶναι τὴν εὐσέβειαν. ⁶ Ἔστιν δὲ πορισμὸς μέγας ἡ εὐσέβεια μετὰ αὐταρκείας· ⁷ οὐδὲν γὰρ εἰσηνέγκαμεν εἰς τὸν κόσμον, ὅτι οὐδὲ ἐξενεγκεῖν τι δυνάμεθα· ⁸ ἔχοντες δὲ διατροφὰς καὶ σκεπάσματα, τούτοις ἀρκεσθησόμεθα. ⁹ οἱ δὲ βουλόμενοι πλουτεῖν ἐμπίπτουσιν εἰς πειρασμὸν καὶ παγίδα καὶ ἐπιθυμίας πολλὰς ἀνοήτους καὶ βλαβεράς, αἵτινες βυθίζουσιν τοὺς ἀνθρώπους εἰς ὄλεθρον καὶ ἀπώλειαν· ¹⁰ ῥίζα γὰρ πάντων τῶν κακῶν ἐστιν ἡ φιλαργυρία, ἧς τινες ὀρεγόμενοι ἀπεπλανήθησαν ἀπὸ τῆς πίστεως καὶ ἑαυτοὺς περιέπειραν ὀδύναις πολλαῖς. ¹¹ Σὺ δέ, ὦ ἄνθρωπε θεοῦ, ταῦτα φεῦγε· δίωκε δὲ δικαιοσύνην εὐσέβειαν πίστιν, ἀγάπην ὑπομονὴν πραϋπαθίαν. ¹² ἀγωνίζου τὸν καλὸν ἀγῶνα τῆς πίστεως, ἐπιλαβοῦ τῆς αἰωνίου ζωῆς, εἰς ἣν ἐκλήθης καὶ ὡμολόγησας τὴν καλὴν ὁμολογίαν ἐνώπιον πολλῶν μαρτύρων. ¹³ παραγγέλλω [σοι] ἐνώπιον τοῦ θεοῦ τοῦ ζῳογονοῦντος τὰ πάντα καὶ Χριστοῦ Ἰησοῦ τοῦ μαρτυρήσαντος ἐπὶ Ποντίου Πιλάτου τὴν καλὴν ὁμολογίαν, ¹⁴ τηρῆσαί σε τὴν ἐντολὴν ἄσπιλον ἀνεπίλημπτον μέχρι τῆς ἐπιφανείας τοῦ κυρίου ἡμῶν Ἰησοῦ Χριστοῦ, ¹⁵ ἣν καιροῖς ἰδίοις δείξει ὁ μακάριος καὶ μόνος δυνάστης, ὁ βασιλεὺς τῶν βασιλευόντων καὶ κύριος τῶν κυριευόντων, ¹⁶ ὁ μόνος ἔχων ἀθανασίαν, φῶς οἰκῶν ἀπρόσιτον, ὃν εἶδεν οὐδεὶς ἀνθρώπων οὐδὲ ἰδεῖν δύναται· ᾧ τιμὴ καὶ κράτος αἰώνιον, ἀμήν. ¹⁷ Τοῖς πλουσίοις ἐν τῷ νῦν αἰῶνι παράγγελλε μὴ ὑψηλοφρονεῖν μηδὲ ἠλπικέναι ἐπὶ πλούτου ἀδηλότητι ἀλλ᾽ ἐπὶ θεῷ τῷ παρέχοντι ἡμῖν πάντα πλουσίως εἰς ἀπόλαυσιν, ¹⁸ ἀγαθοεργεῖν, πλουτεῖν ἐν ἔργοις καλοῖς, εὐμεταδότους εἶναι, κοινωνικούς, ¹⁹ ἀποθησαυρίζοντας ἑαυτοῖς θεμέλιον καλὸν εἰς τὸ μέλλον, ἵνα ἐπιλάβωνται τῆς ὄντως ζωῆς. ²⁰ Ὦ Τιμόθεε, τὴν παραθήκην φύλαξον ἐκτρεπόμενος τὰς βεβήλους κενοφωνίας καὶ ἀντιθέσεις τῆς ψευδωνύμου γνώσεως, ²¹ ἥν τινες ἐπαγγελλόμενοι περὶ τὴν πίστιν ἠστόχησαν. Ἡ χάρις μεθ᾽ ὑμῶν.

³If any one teaches otherwise and does not agree with the sound words of our Lord Jesus Christ and the teaching which accords with godliness, ⁴he is puffed up with conceit, he knows nothing; he has a morbid craving for controversy and for disputes about words, which produce envy, dissension, slander, base suspicions, ⁵and wrangling among men who are depraved in mind and bereft of the truth, imagining that godliness is a means of gain. ⁶There is great gain in godliness with contentment; ⁷for we brought nothing into the world, and we cannot take anything out of the world; ⁸but if we have food and clothing, with these we shall be content. ⁹But those who desire to be rich fall into temptation, into a snare, into many senseless and hurtful desires that plunge men into ruin and destruction. ¹⁰For the love of money is the root of all evils; it is through this craving that some have wandered away from the faith and pierced their hearts with many pangs. ¹¹But as for you, man of God, shun all this; aim at righteousness, godliness, faith, love, steadfastness, gentleness. ¹²Fight the good fight of the faith; take hold of the eternal life to which you were called when you made the good confession in the presence of many witnesses. ¹³In the presence of God who gives life to all things, and of Christ Jesus who in his testimony before Pontius Pilate made the good confession, ¹⁴I charge you to keep the commandment unstained and free from reproach until the appearing of our Lord Jesus Christ; ¹⁵and this will be made manifest at the proper time by the blessed and only Sovereign, the King of kings and Lord of lords, ¹⁶who alone has immortality and dwells in unapproachable light, whom no man has ever seen or can see. To him be honor and eternal dominion. Amen. ¹⁷As for the rich in this world, charge them not to be haughty, nor to set their hopes on uncertain riches but on God

> *who richly furnishes us with everything to enjoy.* ¹⁸*They are to do good, to be rich in good deeds, liberal and generous,* ¹⁹*thus laying up for themselves a good foundation for the future, so that they may take hold of the life which is life indeed.* ²⁰*O Timothy, guard what has been entrusted to you. Avoid the godless chatter and contradictions of what is falsely called knowledge,* ²¹*for by professing it some have missed the mark as regards the faith. Grace be with you.*

At the end of the letter Paul recapitulates what he wrote at the beginning concerning Timothy's responsibility to guard the Apostle's gospel against anyone who would try to adulterate it:[1]

> As I urged (*parekalesa*) you when I was going to Macedonia, remain at Ephesus that you may charge certain persons not to teach any different doctrine (*heterodidaskalein*), nor to occupy themselves with myths and endless genealogies which promote speculations (*ekzētēseis*) rather than the divine training that is *in faith*; whereas the aim of our charge is love that issues from a pure heart and a good conscience and sincere *faith*. Certain persons by swerving from these have wandered away into vain discussion (*mataiologian*), desiring to be teachers of the law, without understanding either what they are saying or the things about which they make assertions. Now we know that the law is good, if any one uses it lawfully, understanding this, that the law is not laid down for the just but for the lawless and disobedient, for the ungodly and sinners, for the unholy and profane, for murderers of fathers and murderers of mothers, for manslayers, immoral persons, sodomites, kidnapers, liars, perjurers, and whatever else is contrary to sound (*hygiainousē*) doctrine (*didaskalia*), in accordance with the glorious gospel of the blessed God with which I have been entrusted. (1 Tim 1:3-11)

---

[1] Just as Paul himself did when writing Galatians: "I am astonished that you are so quickly deserting him who called you in the grace of Christ and turning to a different gospel—not that there is another gospel, but there are some who trouble you and want to pervert the gospel of Christ." (1:6-7)

Teach (*didaske*) and urge (*parakalei*) these duties. If any one teaches otherwise (*heterodidaskalei*) and does not agree with the sound (*hygiainousin*) words of our Lord Jesus Christ and the teaching (*didaskalia*) which accords with godliness (*evsebeian*), he is puffed up with conceit, he knows nothing; he has a morbid craving for controversy (*zēteseis*) and for disputes about words (*logomakhias*), which produce envy, dissension, slander, base suspicions, and wrangling among men who are depraved in mind and bereft of the truth, imagining that godliness (*evsebeian*) is a means of gain. There is great gain in godliness (*evsebeia*) with contentment; for we brought nothing into the world, and we cannot take anything out of the world; but if we have food and clothing, with these we shall be content. But those who desire to be rich fall into temptation, into a snare, into many senseless and hurtful desires that plunge men into ruin and destruction. For the love of money is the root of all evils; it is through this craving that some have wandered away from the *faith* and pierced their hearts with many pangs. (6:2b-10)

The first and main point of interest is that at both the beginning and the end of the letter, Paul underscores that the bishop's main duty is to uphold the "sound" teaching *against* "disputes about words" (*logomakhias*; disputes *with* words) that end up being "vain discussion" (*mataiologian*). He already expressed that thought in his letter to the saints of Colossae, a city of the province Asia whose capital is Ephesus.[2] Moreover, "vain discussion" is described as being led by people "desiring to be teachers of the law, without understanding either what they are saying or the things about which they make assertions" (1 Tim 1:7). Finally, they are said to have "a morbid craving for controversy (*zēteseis*)" (6:4b) based on "speculations (*ekzēteseis*) rather than the divine training that is in faith" (1:4b). Such training would invite the members of the flock to lead a "way of life" according to God's will, which is precisely the "sound" teaching (Col 1:8-11).[3] It is as though Paul foresaw

---

[2] See my comments on Col 2:1-4 in *C-Col* 61-62.
[3] Notice how RSV, in translating here *didaskalia* into "doctrine" rather than "teaching," as it does in 1:10 and 4:6, reflects the pervading "theological" bias toward understanding

1 Timothy: Chapter 6

the rise of philosophical theology. In the first half of the second century "bishops" and leaders of the Christian congregations decided to give priority to Greek philosophical discourse rather than to invite and prod their flock to lead a life that would be to their benefit on judgment day (Mt 25:31-46). The reason for divine training in sound teaching is evident: the judging Son of man (v.31) is none other than the one who summed up his "law" to be followed (Mt 5-7) with the statement:

> Not every one who says to me, "Lord, Lord," shall enter the kingdom of heaven, but he who does the will of my Father who is in heaven. On that day many will say to me, "Lord, Lord, did we not prophesy in your name, and cast out demons in your name, and do many mighty works in your name?" And then will I declare to them, "I never knew you; depart from me, you evildoers." (7:21-23)

Unfortunately, as Paul foresaw, the path of philosophical theology led to "envy, dissension (*eris*), slander, base suspicions, and wrangling among men" (1 Tim 6:4) all of which were strictly forbidden by Paul.[4] The most notable example of such dissension is the aftermath of the Council of Chacedon that unwarrantedly tore apart the Christian East less than four centuries after the mission of unity between Jew and Gentile was championed by Jesus and Paul (Gal 2:1-14; Eph 2:11-22).

The repeated mention of godliness (*evsebeian*; 1 Tim 6:3, 5, 6) in the entire passage (vv.2a-10) confirms that "sound" teaching has to do with behavior rather than with a mental theoretical creed concerning the deity. The seriousness of this matter is evident from the use of the Hebrew *kabbed*, translated as "honor" (*timan*); it is the same verb that means "glorify" when used with God as its complement. Honoring one's elders is tantamount to honoring

---

pistis as a "creed" versus its original meaning of "trust" in God that his commandments for us to obey and live by are for our *own* good and, ultimately, salvation.
[4] See especially 1 Corinthians 1:11; 3:3; 12:20.

God, the ultimate parent. This is the well-known Greek *evsebeia* and Latin *pietas*, the required attitude of reverence toward one's "seniors," be they gods,[5] elders, or even those who are deceased. The opposite, Greek *asebeia* or Latin *impietas*, is "wickedness," which is despicable in scripture.[6] It was assumed that one was "blessed" so long as one was "pious," which explains why this title was linked with the rulers. The gods would protect a ruler so long as he showed "piety." The parallelism in meaning between "honor" and "godliness" is further borne out in the required behavior toward widows, who are obviously seniors. Their children, and Timothy as well, are to "honor (*tima*) widows who are real widows. If a widow has children or grandchildren, let them first learn *their religious duty to* (*evsebein*; to reverence) their own family and make some return to their parents; for this is acceptable in the sight of God." (5:2-3) Such behavior is befitting of a junior toward a senior.

---

[5] Hence *theosebeia* (reverence toward the gods) as in 1 Tim 2:10: "... but by good deeds, as befits women who profess religion (*theosebeian*)."

[6] The equation of ungodliness with wickedness is borne out in Romans where Paul compares the sin of ungodliness among the nations with that of wickedness—unlawfulness—among the Jews. In preparation for Romans 2, where he is going to include the Jews in the de facto infringement of God's will in spite of their knowledge thereof, in Romans 1 Paul dubs the sin of men not only as "ungodliness" (*asebeian*) but also as "wickedness" (*adikia*; unlawfulness) (1:18); *asebeia* (Latin *impietas*) is a classic term in Greco-Roman society, whose positive counterpart is *evsebeia* (Latin *pietas*). Being "pious" means to have reverence primarily toward the gods, but equally toward the dead and the elders. Thus, *evsebeia* amounts to the respect due to those in a higher position compared to us; *asebeia* is the lack of such reverence. The generalization of the sin of "ungodliness" to "all men" goes hand in hand with that the first "word" or "commandment" in the Decalogue pertaining to our relation to other human being is: "Honor (Hebrew *kabbed*; Greek *tima*) your father and your mother, *that your days may be long* in the land which the Lord your God gives you" (Ex 20:12); "Honor (Hebrew *kabbed*; Greek *tima*) your father and your mother, as the Lord your God commanded you; *that your days may be prolonged, and that it may go well with you*, in the land which the Lord your God gives you." (Deut 5:16) By the same token, when viewed scripturally, the *asebeia* becomes also *adikia* (unlawfulness; unrighteousness; wickedness), thus applying in a specific way to the Jew.

1 Timothy: Chapter 6

The sudden switch from the ungodliness of the false teaching (6:3) to the ungodliness of the pursuit of earthly riches (vv.6-10) seems perplexing. Soon enough, however, the general statement of verses 1-6 referring to "any one" (*tis*; v.3) is taken up in the specific address to Timothy (But as for you, man of God; v.11). It starts with the godliness of the true faith (v.11) requiring the "good fight" (v.12a) expressed in the "good confession in the presence of many witnesses" (v.12b), similar to that "of Christ Jesus before Pontius Pilate" (v.13). It ends with a similar admonition against "the rich in this world" (vv.17-19). Thus the concern with earthly riches is essential to the entire spirit of the concluding chapter of a letter dedicated to the "sound teaching"[7] (1:10; 6:3) since the pursuit of earthly riches is presented as a prime example of, if not outright tantamount to, ungodliness.

A close analysis of the vocabulary and phraseology of the chapter will allow us to understand its message as well as the scriptural validity of this argument. A point of departure would be verses 5-6 that form a hinge between the two sections dealing with the false teaching (vv.1-5) and the love of money (vv.6-10) by using the same pair "godliness-gain" in an inverted manner:[8] "... and wrangling among men who are depraved in mind and bereft of the truth, imagining that godliness (*evsebeian*) is a means of gain (*porismon*). There is great gain (*porismon*) in godliness (*evsebeia*) with contentment." One encounters here the only occurrences of the root *poriz*— (*porism*—) in the New Testament. Elsewhere in

---

[7] RSV has "sound doctrine." See earlier my comments on this ill-advised misleading translation.
[8] The inversion is a literary pattern where the sequence of the pair of words is switched (godliness [A] gain [B], gain [A'] godliness [B']) which is used to underscore to the ear the intended link between two related statements.

scripture, it is only in the Book of Wisdom that we find this same root, where it is used in a context contrasting God with the idols:[9]

> For health he[10] appeals to a thing that is weak; for life he prays to a thing that is dead; for aid he entreats a thing that is utterly inexperienced; for a prosperous journey, a thing that cannot take a step; for money-making (*porismou*) and work and success with his hands he asks strength of a thing whose hands have no strength. Again, one preparing to sail and about to voyage over raging waves calls upon a piece of wood more fragile than the ship which carries him. For it was desire for gain (*porismōn*) that planned that vessel, and wisdom was the craftsman who built it; but it is thy providence, O Father, that steers its course, because thou hast given it a path in the sea, and a safe way through the waves, showing that thou canst save from every danger, so that even if a man lacks skill, he may put to sea. It is thy will that works of thy wisdom should not be without effect; therefore men trust their lives even to the smallest piece of wood, and passing through the billows on a raft they come safely to land. (13:18-14:5)

One can safely surmise that 1Timothy had this passage in mind since the specific address to Timothy as bishop ends with a summons that underscores God's sole true richness versus the false richness of the wealthy:

> In the presence of God who gives life to all things, and of Christ Jesus who in his testimony before Pontius Pilate made the good confession, I charge you to keep the commandment unstained and free from reproach until the appearing of our Lord Jesus Christ; and this will be made manifest at the proper time by the blessed and only Sovereign, the King of kings and Lord of lords, who alone has immortality and dwells in unapproachable light, whom no man has ever seen or can see. To him be honor and eternal dominion. Amen.

---

[9] "But miserable, with their hopes set on dead things, are the men who give the name "gods" to the works of men's hands, gold and silver fashioned with skill, and likenesses of animals, or a useless stone, the work of an ancient hand." (13:10)

[10] The "skilled woodcutter" of 13:11.

As for the rich (*plousiois*) in this world, charge them not to be haughty, nor to set their hopes on uncertain riches (*ploutou*) but on God who richly (*plousiōs*) furnishes us with everything to enjoy. They are to do good, to be rich (*ploutein*) in good deeds, liberal and generous (1 Tim 6:13-18)

When one further considers the reference to God as "the King of kings" (v.15) and is aware that *melek*, the Hebrew original for king, literally means "proprietor, owner," then the message is clear. A city's monarch was, by definition, the *sole* owner of that city and all its possessions; thus the monarch was the rich person par excellence. Yet the riches of God as king makes of any other wealth merely "uncertain riches" (*ploutou adēlotēti* [wealth of uncertainty]; v.17). This thought is an essential component of the letter since it brackets it as an *inclusio*: "*To the King of ages*, immortal, invisible, the only God, be honor and glory for ever and ever. Amen." (1:17) The closeness in thought is further evident in the oneness of God as King in both cases: "the only (*monō*) God" (1:17) and "and this will be made manifest at the proper time by the blessed and only (*monos*) Sovereign, the King of kings and Lord of lords, who alone (*monos*) has immortality" (6:15-16). These are the only instances of the adjectival *monos* in the letter.[11]

Unlike the Book of Wisdom where the text reflects an attack on the idols, here in 1 Timothy God's nemeses are the wealthy human beings. In the Roman empire the wealthy were usually patresfamilias, that is, heads of household patricians, who could wield undue influence on the running of the Pauline household churches. Timothy, as bishop, should do his utmost to keep such

---

[11] Elsewhere we have once the adverb *monon*: "Besides that, they learn to be idlers, gadding about from house to house, and not only (*ou monon*) idlers but also (*alla kai*) gossips and busybodies, saying what they should not." (5:13)

people in check under the authority of God who ultimately is the sole paterfamilias within the confines of the household churches:

> He [the bishop] must manage his own household well, keeping his children submissive and respectful in every way; for if a man does not know how to manage his own household, how can he care for God's church? (1 Tim 3:4-5)

One finds the same thought in the letter to the church of Ephesus where Timothy was bishop (1:1):

> For this reason I bow my knees before the Father, from whom every family (*patria*; domain of a father; fatherhood) in heaven and on earth is named ... one God and Father of us all, who is above all and through all and in all. (Eph 3:14-15; 4:6)

Since this God and Father is "invisible" (*aoratō*; 1 Tim 1:17) and thus "whom no man has ever seen or can see" (6:16), he de facto functions as the absent master who left the care of his household to his chief steward:

> And the Lord said, "Who then is the faithful and wise steward (*oikonomos*), whom his master will set over his household, to give them their portion of food at the proper time? Blessed is that servant whom his master when he comes will find so doing. Truly, I say to you, he will set him over all his possessions. But if that servant says to himself, 'My master is delayed in coming,' and begins to beat the menservants and the maidservants, and to eat and drink and get drunk, the master of that servant will come on a day when he does not expect him and at an hour he does not know, and will punish him, and put him with the unfaithful. And that servant who knew his master's will, but did not make ready or act according to his will, shall receive a severe beating. But he who did not know, and did what deserved a beating, shall receive a light beating. Every one to whom much is given, of him will much be required; and of him to whom men commit much they will demand the more." (Lk 12:42-48)

Therefore, in the "visual" absence of God, the bishop is to care for the church, God's "household" (1 Tim 3:4-5), as the accountable steward: "For a bishop, as God's steward (*oikonomon*), must be blameless." (Tit 1:7a) In 1 Timothy, the bishop's commission is referred to as *oikonomia*, the duty of an *oikonomos*: "As I urged you when I was going to Macedonia, remain at Ephesus that you may charge certain persons not to teach any different doctrine, nor to occupy themselves with myths and endless genealogies which promote speculations rather than the *divine training* (*oikonomian theou*; charge[12] given by God to his *oikonomos*) that is in faith; whereas the aim of our charge (*parangelias*) is love that issues from a pure heart and a good conscience and sincere faith." (1:3-5) That love for the needy junior, as in the Lukan parable, is the antidote to the arrogance of "assumed" riches is evident in that the element "love" brackets the letter: "But as for you, man of God, shun all this; aim at (*diōke*; [earnestly] pursue) righteousness, godliness, faith, love, steadfastness, gentleness." (6:11).

Moreover, such love is not an option, but rather an apostolic "charge" (*parangelias*; 1:5) as is clear from its subsequent mention: "This charge (*parangelian*) I commit to you, Timothy, my son, in accordance with the prophetic utterances which pointed to you." (v.18a) Furthermore, this apostolic charge is no less than a divine "commandment" for which we all shall be accountable:[13]

> I charge (*parangellō*) you to keep (*tērēsai*) the commandment (*entolēn*) unstained and free from reproach until the appearing of our Lord Jesus Christ; and this will be made manifest at the proper time by the blessed and only Sovereign, the King of kings and Lord of lords, who alone has immortality and dwells in unapproachable

---

[12] Notice how this commission is referred to in the following verse as "charge" (*parangelias*).
[13] See also 1 Cor 7:10: "To the married I give charge (*parangellō*), *not I but the Lord*, that the wife should not separate from her husband."

light, whom no man has ever seen or can see. To him be honor and eternal dominion. Amen. (6:14-16)

This statement follows Paul's request to "Fight the good fight of the *faith*; take hold of the eternal life to which you were called when you made *the good confession (tēn kalēn homologian) in the presence of (enōpion)* many witnesses *(martyrōn)*" (v.12a), which is linked to the preceding "aim at righteousness, godliness, *faith, love*, steadfastness, gentleness" (v.11), where faith is coupled with love at the center of the six-fold request. The request of verse 13 begins with the same phraseology as the ending of the preceding verse: "*In the presence of (enōpion)* God who gives life to all things, and of Christ Jesus who in his testimony *(martyrēsantos)* before Pontius Pilate made *the good confession (tēn kalēn homologian)*" (v.13). This, in turn, introduces the apostolic charge of verse 14. The conclusion is compelling: the commandment to be kept is none other than the commandment of love that lies at the heart of the Pauline gospel as expressed in the earlier letter written to the Galatians:

> For through the Spirit, by faith, we wait for the hope of righteousness. For in Christ Jesus neither circumcision nor uncircumcision is of any avail, but faith working through love. (5:5-6)

> For you were called to freedom, brethren; only do not use your freedom as an opportunity for the flesh, but through love be servants of one another. For the whole law is fulfilled in one word, "You shall love your neighbor as yourself." But if you bite and devour one another take heed that you are not consumed by one another. (vv.13-15)[14]

---

[14] See also Rom 13:8-10.

But the fruit of the Spirit is love, joy, peace, patience, kindness, goodness, faithfulness, gentleness, self-control; against such there is no law. (vv.22-23)

The "commandment" of "love" having a divine source, that is to say, being scriptural, and not merely of apostolic origin, finds support in the Johannine epistles:

> Beloved, I am writing you no new commandment, but an old commandment which you had from the beginning; the old commandment is the word which you have heard. Yet I am writing you a new commandment, which is true in him and in you, because the darkness is passing away and the true light is already shining. He who says he is in the light and hates his brother is in the darkness still. He who loves his brother abides in the light, and in it there is no cause for stumbling. But he who hates his brother is in the darkness and walks in the darkness, and does not know where he is going, because the darkness has blinded his eyes. (1 Jn 2:7-11)

> By this we shall know that we are of the truth, and reassure our hearts before him whenever our hearts condemn us; for God is greater than our hearts, and he knows everything. Beloved, if our hearts do not condemn us, we have confidence before God; and we receive from him whatever we ask, because we keep his commandments and do what pleases him. And this is his commandment, that we should believe in the name of his Son Jesus Christ and love one another, just as he has commanded us. All who keep (*tērōn*: from the same verb *tērēsai* of 1 Tim 6:14) his commandments abide in him, and he in them. And by this we know that he abides in us, by the Spirit which he has given us. (3:19-24)

> We love, because he first loved us. If any one says, "I love God," and hates his brother, he is a liar; for he who does not love his brother whom he has seen (*heōraken*), cannot love God whom he has not seen (*heōraken*).[15] And this commandment we have from him, that he who loves God should love his brother also. (4:19-21)

---

[15] *heōraken* is from the same root *aoratō* (invisible) of 1 Tim 1:17.

> I rejoiced greatly to find some of your children following the truth, just as we have been commanded by the Father. And now I beg you, lady, not as though I were writing you a new commandment, but the one we have had from the beginning, that we love one another. And this is love, that we follow his commandments; this is the commandment, as you have heard from the beginning, that you follow love. (2 Jn 1:4-6)

Further confirmation is found in 1 Timothy itself. This letter is bracketed with the rarely used verb *astokhein* (swerve [1:6]; miss the mark [6:21]) that occurs in the New Testament only a third time in the companion letter 2 Timothy.[16] In 1 Timothy 1:6, *astokhein* is used directly in conjunction with "love":

> As I urged you when I was going to Macedonia, remain at Ephesus that you may charge certain persons not to teach any different doctrine (teaching), nor to occupy themselves with myths and endless genealogies which promote speculations rather than the divine training (*oikonomian*; house management) that is in faith; whereas the aim of our charge is love that issues from a pure heart and a good conscience and sincere faith. Certain persons by swerving from these have wandered away into vain discussion, desiring to be teachers of the law, without understanding either what they are saying or the things about which they make assertions. (1:3-7)

Instead of heeding Paul's caveat, classical theology, launched by a number of Greek intelligentsia that joined the "Way" (Acts 9:2; 19:9, 23; 22:4; 24:14, 22), started dealing with this teaching as an intellectual pursuit in search of the ultimate truth about God, thus perceiving it to be a mental reality instead of a behavioral path that one treads out of trust (*pistis*) in the one who is "calling" us to obey

---

[16] "Among them are Hymenaeus and Philetus, who have swerved (*ēstokhēsan*) from the truth by holding that the resurrection is past already. They are upsetting the faith of some." (2 Tim 2:17b-18a)

his message and follow his will embedded therein. Even more, as the apostle wrote:

> Therefore, my beloved, as you have always obeyed, so now, not only as in my presence but much more in my absence, work out your own salvation with fear and trembling; for God is at work in you, both to will and to work for his good pleasure. (Phil 2:12-13)

Tradition and Deposit

I should like to clarify a common misnomer in classical theology regarding "living tradition" which is generally understood as the carrying on of the tradition of the apostles across the centuries through the medium of "holy persons" who teach and live the gospel preached by those apostles. First of all, the phrase "living tradition" is nowhere to be found in the New Testament. The closest one can get is "living … in accord with the tradition (*paradosin*) that you received from us [the apostles, namely Paul]" (2 Thess 3:6). The original for "living" is *peripatountos*, which means "walking" and thus "behaving." More importantly, though, is the fact that the "tradition" (*paradosis*) is by definition apostolic. It starts and ends with the apostle, just as the "word of the Lord" was poured as "words" into the mouth of the prophet (Jer 1:9) and ended up deposited as "written words" to live by, rather than as words to be elaborated upon by subsequent generations (Jer 36). That is why the verb "deliver" (*paradidōmi*) as well as the cognate noun "tradition" (*paradosis*), which abound in the Pauline letters to communities, disappear in his letters to the "bishop" Timothy, and are replaced with the verb *paratithemai* (commit, entrust) and the cognate noun *parathēkē* (deposit [not to be tampered with]). The "tradition" settles into an apostolic letter as the "deposit" which is handed down throughout the generations *as* deposit, and not *as* tradition. This is evident in Paul's admonitions to Timothy. He *commits* this charge to Timothy who, in turn, is then to *entrust* to others:

> This charge (*parangelian*) I commit (*paratithemai*) to you, Timothy, my son (1 Tim 1:18a)

> You then, my son, be strong in the grace that is in Christ Jesus, and what you have heard from me before many witnesses entrust (*parathou*, imperative of the verb *paratithemai*) to faithful men who will be able to teach others also. (2 Tim 2:1-2)

That is why the "deposit" (*parathēkē*) is to be "kept" both in the sense of being "lived by" as well as being "preserved." Both of these connotations are borne out in the original text through the use of *phylassō*:

> O Timothy, guard (*phylaxon*) what has been entrusted (*tēn parathēkēn*) to you (1 Tim 6:20).

> Guard (*phylaxon*) [the truth][17] that has been entrusted (*tēn kalēn parathēkēn* [the good deposit]) to you by the Holy Spirit who dwells within[18] us (2 Tim 1:14).

In 1 Corinthians (3:5-9) Paul writes that it is God himself who controls the growth of the plant that was seeded and watered by his co-workers, the ministers of the gospel. He writes to Timothy that God "is able to guard until that Day what has been entrusted to me (*tēn parathēkēn mou*)" (2 Tim 1:12). In turn, Timothy is to guard the deposit entrusted[19] to him and to hand it *as deposit* to his followers: "Follow the pattern of the sound words which you have heard from me, in faith and love which are in Christ Jesus; guard the truth that has been entrusted to you." (v.14).

---

[17] Not in the original.
[18] The meaning of the original is "among" rather than "in."
[19] My translation. RSV distorts the original by making it sound as though God handed Paul a "deposit": "But I am not ashamed, for I know whom I have believed, and I am sure that he is able to guard until that Day what has been entrusted to me." (2 Tim 1:12). Rather, God commissioned Paul with the gospel (Gal 1:11-17; 2:7-9; Rom 1:1-2; 1 Cor 15:1-11) which he, Paul, then committed as deposited writ in his letters.

1 Timothy: Chapter 6 103

This written deposit preserved *as scripture* in the Pauline letters is validated in 2 Peter:

> Therefore, beloved, since you wait for these, be zealous to be found by him without spot (*aspiloi*) or blemish, and at peace. And count the forbearance of our Lord as salvation. *So also our beloved brother Paul wrote to you according to the wisdom given him, speaking* (*lalōn*) *of this as he does in all his letters* (*epistolais*). There are some things in them hard to understand, which the ignorant and unstable twist to their own destruction (*apōleia*), *as they do the other scriptures.* You therefore, beloved, knowing this beforehand, beware (*phylassesthe*; guard yourselves) lest you be carried away with the error of lawless men and lose your own stability. But grow in the grace and knowledge of our Lord and Savior Jesus Christ. To him be the glory both now and to the day of eternity. Amen. (3:14-18)

The closeness between this passage in 2 Peter and 1 Timothy 6 is evident in their similar terminology. The term *aspiloi* (without spot) is restricted in the New Testament to 1 Peter (1:19), 2 Peter (3:14), 1 Timothy (6:14) and James (1:27). The noun *apōleia* (destruction), a staple of 2 Peter,[20] occurs only once in the Pastoral Epistles in 1 Timothy 6:9. The verb *phylassein* (keep; guard), which abounds in 1 and 2 Timothy is found only in the above quoted ending of 2 Peter.[21] This same passage "scripturalizes" the letters of Paul by putting them on par with "the other scriptures," that is to say, at least the Old Testament, if not also the Gospels.[22] Moreover, by using the verb *lalōn*, which is the verb that Paul uses when referring to his preaching the gospel, the author of 2 Peter is underscoring the fact that Paul's "oral gospel" is to be found exclusively in his epistles rather than in any assumed "oral tradition." In other words, Paul's "oral gospel" is handed down

---

[20] 2 Pet 2:1 (twice), 3; 3:7, 16.
[21] The exception being in a totally different connotation: "If he [God] did not spare the ancient world, but preserved (*ephylaxen*) Noah, a herald of righteousness, with seven other persons, when he brought a flood upon the world of the ungodly." (2 Pet 2:5)
[22] See my comments on Col 4:7-18 in *C-Col* 94-106.

through the ages *in his letters*. This was the case in his earlier letter written to the Galatians. What Paul had "said before," he is "again saying" (1:9) in "the *grammata* (the actual written alphabetical letters) he is writing with his own hand" (6:11). The centrality of this thought is evident in that Paul uses this formula no less than four times (1 Cor 16:21; Gal 6:11; Col 4:18; 2 Thess 3:17), the last of which is all encompassing: "I, Paul, write this greeting with my own hand. This is the mark in every letter (*epistolē*; epistle) of mine; it is the way I write."

Consequently, Timothy, and much less his followers, is not given a free reign to carry on a supposedly "living tradition." He is not allowed to add his own thoughts and twists to the *written* apostolic legacy. The "foundation" laid by Paul alone functions as muster against which even the work of his colleague Barnabas, let alone Timothy, will be judged (1 Cor 3:10-15). Even more. Anyone who, through his own input, "destroys" (*phtheirei*; brings to naught through perversion) that work, "God will destroy (*phtheirei*; bring to naught) him" (v.17). That is why, just as Timothy "from childhood has been acquainted with the sacred writings[23] [the Old Testament] which are able to instruct him for salvation" (2 Tim 3:15), so he is to acquaint himself not so much with what he has "heard" from Paul, but rather with Paul's "letters" (2 Pet 3:16). The strictness in adhering to this directive is incontrovertible, and the New Testament canon affirms this: its writings include those of Paul's nemeses, James, Cephas/Peter, and John, the pillars of the Jerusalem meeting (Gal 2:9)—yet a *writing* by Timothy, the bishop at the Pauline headquarters in Ephesus, is nowhere to be found! He is as much absent from the canon as he was from the Jerusalem meeting! All he can do is use the sacred writings, new as well as old, to feed the flock *out of these*. And if the New Testament canon relegates Timothy to a

---

[23] Instead of *graphas* (scriptures) the original has *grammata* which are the actual written alphabetical letters. Thus the stress is on the actual writ of the writers themselves.

secondary position, much more so are those bishops and church leaders who follow after him. Their writings are in no way an authoritative explanation of scripture, but are to be continually tested against the Holy Writ that alone is officially heard in the congregations. Only scripture contains the divine "voice" to be obeyed throughout all the generations.[24] The proclivity to aggrandize our predecessors is not only Greco-Roman, but universal as well. However, it is in no way scriptural. Actually, it is anti-scriptural! Scripture consistently declaims the "sins" of the forebears rather than their obedience, while in the same breath upholds the perennial validity of the perennially contravened commandments. The classic passage of this scriptural stand is the preamble to Psalm 78:

> Give ear, O my people, to my teaching; incline your ears to the words of my mouth! I will open my mouth in a parable; I will utter dark sayings from of old, things that we have heard and known, that our fathers have told us. We will not hide them from their children, but tell to the coming generation the glorious deeds of the Lord, and his might, and the wonders which he has wrought. He established a testimony in Jacob, and appointed a law in Israel, which he commanded our fathers *to teach to their children*; that *the next generation* might know them, the children yet unborn, and *arise and tell them to their children*, so that they should *set their hope in God*, and not forget the works of God, but keep his commandments; *and* that they should *not be like their fathers*, a stubborn and rebellious generation, a generation whose heart was not steadfast, whose spirit was not faithful to God. (vv.1-8)

Absenteeism versus Divine Invisibility

Before proceeding to 2 Timothy, I should like to visit in more detail the matter of God's invisibility (1 Tim 1:17), and thus "whom no man has ever seen or can see" (6:16), and to relate this

---

[24] See my comments on this subject in *C-Jer* 57-78.

to the function of the bishop as the house manager in the absence of the house master.

God's invisibility in scripture is tantamount to his *voluntary* absence and is no way to be construed in terms of a philosophical *essential* quality or feature. This is actually an impossibility. Linguistically speaking, Hebrew has no equivalent to the Greek *ousia* (being, essence) and the Latin *essentia*. Both *ousia* and *essentia* are nouns reflecting the verb "to be" (Greek *einai*; Latin *esse*), and thus assume the use of such verb in the "present" tense. Hebrew, however, has no equivalent for the "present" tense, nor any other grammatical tense for that matter. Its two main conjugations, as is the case in all Semitic languages, are built not on the basis of time, but rather from the perspective of the action, which can be either already consummated or in the process of taking place.[25] Consequently, the "present" tense of the verb "to be" is rendered through the "nominal sentence" where a subject matter (noun) is immediately followed by either another noun or an adjective describing its "status." Nominal sentences—without the verb "to be"—are a staple of both the Greek and Latin languages,[26] where the addition of "is" to link the "subject" and the "predicate" is optional, and thus unnecessary for the meaning of the statement. That is why the entire debate as to whether someone or something *is* in the sense of *exists* by definition is an oxymoron since the mere mention of a subject matter as a predicate assumes its existence for the speaker. Therefore, stating that someone or something *is* or *exists* is as oxymoronic as stating that the same *is not* or *does not exist*. In the first case, why stress the existence of someone or something you are speaking of, and conversely why try to deny the existence of someone or something after having yourself assumed their existence through the mere fact of mentioning them? In the

---

[25] This approach to verbal conjugation is more realistic since one cannot speak of an action *before* its start (past tense) unless one has witnessed that start, nor can one vouchsafe that an action will *for sure* take place (future tense).
[26] It is still to be heard in Slavic languages.

latter case, why are you even speaking of "them" or, more pertinently, whom and what are you talking about?

Given this logical as well as linguistic premise, *in scripture* God is not only a given, but an essential component of, if not outright the main agent in, the scriptural story. In order to test our resolve to follow his commandments even when he is "turning his back," so to speak, he repeatedly plays the role of the absentee landlord. The most pertinent example of this is in the parable quoted earlier (Lk 12:42-48). "Playing the role" should be taken at face value since the original meaning of the Greek *prosōpon* and the Latin *persona* refers to the mask that an actor donned to play a role on the stage.[27] Unfortunately, theology made of *prosōpon* an actual "person." The original connotation is evident in the Septuagint's opting for *prosōpon* to render the original Hebrew *panim* whose meaning is "face," and thus how someone *appears* when facing the others. Since the deity, any deity, is per definition a judge of its subjects, the scriptural God is the judge par excellence as is clear from Psalm 82 where he judges even the other deities:

A Psalm of Asaph.

God has taken his place in the divine council; in the midst of the gods he holds judgment: "How long will you judge unjustly and show partiality to the wicked? [Selah] Give justice to the weak and the fatherless; maintain the right of the afflicted and the destitute. Rescue the weak and the needy; deliver them from the hand of the wicked." They have neither knowledge nor understanding, they walk about in darkness; all the foundations of the earth are shaken. I say, "You are gods, sons of the Most High, all of you; nevertheless, you shall die like men, and fall like any prince." Arise, O God, judge the earth; for to thee belong all the nations!

---

[27] This understanding is reflected in our English "persona," connoting the character of a "person."

The connotation of a judging presence linked to *panim* is corroborated in that the Hebrew for the adverb "before" or the adverbial phrase "in front of" is either *liphne* (to the face [*panim*] of) or *le'ene* (to the eyes of). That is to say, being "before" is practically equivalent to being "in the presence of" and, more specifically, "standing before" or "being under scrutiny." This, in turn, explains why the two most common Hebrew nouns for "ire" or "wrath" are *ḥemah* (heat) and, more so, *'aph* (nose). The nose is more pertinent for our discussion since it is the prominent organ of the face, which appears as "(nostrils) fuming (with heat)" in the classic graphic depiction of divine ire. Thus the "face" of God connoted his presence *as judge* since that same face can turn into a "nose" at any given moment if what the divine "eyes" see is unsatisfactory. Given this ambivalence pertaining to the "presence" of a judge, an absence on his part carries with it a sense of relief among those who would otherwise be "standing before" the judgment seat. Consequently, *in scripture*, the absence of God as the master who is away is not to be construed in negative terms as though he does not care for us. To the contrary, God recedes *on purpose* to the background *as an expression of his mercy*, and sends us his emissaries and representatives whose mission is to remind us of his will. This allows us extra time to repent of our unsatisfactory behavior so that, whenever he "comes back," "becomes present," we would be found as "righteously innocent" as Christ. That is why, at the *beginning* of his first letter Peter writes:

> Therefore gird up your minds, be sober, set your hope fully upon the grace that is coming to you at the revelation of Jesus Christ. As obedient children, do not be conformed to the passions of your former ignorance, but as he who called you is holy, be holy yourselves in all your conduct; since it is written, "You shall be holy, for I am holy." *And if you invoke as Father him who judges each one impartially according to his deeds, conduct yourselves with fear throughout the time of your exile.* You know that you were ransomed

from the futile ways inherited from your fathers, not with perishable things such as silver or gold, but with the precious blood of Christ, like that of a lamb without blemish (*amōmou*) or spot (*aspilou*). He was destined before the foundation of the world *but was made manifest at the end of the times for your sake*. Through him you have confidence in God, who raised him from the dead and gave him glory, so that your faith and hope are in God. (1 Pet 1:13-21)

Whereas, at the closing of his second letter, and thus bracketing his entire message, he concludes with the warning:

Since all these things are thus to be dissolved, what sort of persons ought you to be in lives of holiness and godliness, *waiting for* and hastening *the coming of the day of God*, because of which the heavens will be kindled and dissolved, and *the elements will melt with fire*! But according to his promise we wait for new heavens and a new earth *in which righteousness dwells*. Therefore, beloved, *since you wait for these*, be zealous to be found by him without spot (*aspiloi*) or blemish (*amōmētoi*),[28] and at peace. And *count the forbearance of our Lord as salvation*. (2 Pet 3:11-15a)

It is no wonder then that, immediately thereafter, Peter recommends:

So also our beloved brother Paul wrote to you according to the wisdom given him, speaking of this as he does in all his letters. There are some things in them hard to understand, which the ignorant and unstable twist to their own destruction, as they do the other scriptures. (vv.15b-16)

Indeed, it is Paul himself who used the third instance of *aspilos* in the New Testament in addressing earlier the bishop (*episkopos*) Timothy: "I charge you to keep (*tērein*) the commandment unstained (*aspilon*) and free from reproach until the appearing of our Lord Jesus Christ." (1 Tim 6:14) His teaching finds resonance

---

[28] The pair *aspilos* and *amōmos/ētos* occurs only in these two instances in the New Testament.

in a passage that uses the fourth and only instance of *aspilos* in the New Testament and, no less, at the hand of Paul's nemesis, James: "If any one thinks he is religious, and does not bridle his tongue but deceives his heart, this man's religion is vain. Religion that is pure and undefiled *before God and the Father* is this: to visit (*episkeptesthai*; from the same root as *episkopos*) orphans and widows in their affliction, and to keep (*tērein*) oneself unstained (*aspilon*) from the world." (Jas 1:26-27) Both Paul and James are at one in underscoring that the ultimate test on judgment day is the care for the needy neighbor. This message will be immortalized in Matthew (25:31-46), the last book of the New Testament to be written by the Pauline school.

By delving into the vain discussion of divine "essential" invisibility and making of it a conundrum to be solved through the "incarnation," theology practically voided the "urgency" of the gospel message: God absented himself for a while in order to test our resolve to abide by his will *while he is absent*. This is precisely his touch of grace since his "presence" may well reveal itself as a "(fuming) nose" rather than a "face," a "(well-meaning) countenance." This is why his emissary Paul, who is not the judge but a mere teacher of the divine law, warns the Philippians to emulate Christ, the consummate divine emissary and teacher in his consummate obedience to his God and Father:

> So if there is any encouragement in Christ, any incentive of love, any participation in the Spirit, any affection and sympathy, complete my joy by being of the same mind, having the same love, being in full accord and of one mind. Do nothing from selfishness or conceit, but in humility count others better than yourselves. Let each of you look not only to his own interests, but also to the interests of others. Have this mind among yourselves, which is yours in Christ Jesus, who, though he was in the form of God, did not count equality with God a thing to be grasped, but emptied himself, taking the form of a servant (*doulou*; slave), being born in the likeness of men. And being found in human form he humbled

himself and *became obedient* unto death, even death on a cross. Therefore God has highly exalted him and bestowed on him the name which is above every name, that at the name of Jesus every knee should bow, in heaven and on earth and under the earth, and every tongue confess that Jesus Christ is Lord, to the glory of God the Father. Therefore, my beloved, as *you have always obeyed*, so now, not only as *in my presence* but *much more in my absence*, work out your own salvation with fear and trembling; for God is at work in you, both to will and to work for his good pleasure. (Phil 2:1-13)

The gospel is an invitation to the Gentiles to obediently follow God's law *already handed down* in the Old Testament (Rom 1:1-2) and entrusted to Israel (3:2). The Gentile intelligentsia that "turned to Christ" revamped that gospel message using the philosophical lingo of Plato, Aristotle, Philo, Justin the Philosopher, Origen, Plotinus, and the like, and turned it into a mental discourse, something that was strictly forbidden by Paul. In both Colossians and 1 Timothy, after having stated that the gospel word (*logos*) revolves around doing God's will, which is for us to be merciful unto the needy others just as God himself behaves toward us,[29] Paul purposely uses terminology woven around the root *logos* to describe the cunning perversion of the gospel word. Earlier he wrote to the Galatians: "I am astonished that you are so quickly deserting him who called you in the grace of Christ and turning to a different gospel—not that there is another gospel, but there are some who trouble you and want to pervert the gospel of Christ." (Gal 1:6-7)

In Colossians he writes, "And so, from the day we heard of it, we have not ceased to pray for you, asking that you may be filled with *the knowledge of his will* in all spiritual wisdom and understanding, *to lead a life worthy of the Lord, fully pleasing to him, bearing fruit in every good work* and increasing in the knowledge of

---

[29] See especially Rom 5:1-11. See also the Matthean parable of the unmerciful servant (Mt 18:23-35).

God."³⁰ (1:9-10) Then he proceeds to write in the following chapters:

> For I want you to know how greatly I strive for you, and for those at Laodicea, and for all who have not seen my face, *that their hearts may be encouraged as they are knit together in love*, to have all the riches of assured understanding and the knowledge of God's mystery, of Christ, in whom are hid all the treasures of wisdom and knowledge. I say this in order that no one may delude (*paralogizetai*; speaks in a manner to skirt the true gospel word)³¹ you with beguiling speech (*pithanologia*). (2:1-4)

> In these *you once walked*, when *you lived in them*. But now put them all away: anger, wrath, malice, slander, and foul talk (*aiskhrologian*) from your mouth. (3:7-8)

He follows a similar strategy in 1 Timothy:

> As I urged you when I was going to Macedonia, remain at Ephesus that you may charge certain persons not to teach any different doctrine, nor to occupy themselves with myths and endless genealogies (*genealogiais*) which promote speculations rather than the divine training that is in faith; whereas *the aim of our charge is love* that issues from a pure heart and a good conscience and sincere faith. Certain persons by swerving from these have wandered away into vain discussion (*mataiologian*), desiring to be teachers of the law, without understanding either what they are saying or the things about which they make assertions. (1:3-7)

---

[30] As I pointed out in *C-Col* 40-42 "the knowledge of God" is a shortened formula for "the knowledge of God's will" (v.9) and does in no way refer to an intellectual knowledge, which would amount to human (Greek) wisdom that is openly criticized in 1 Cor 1-3.

[31] Notice the use of the same preposition *para* twice in a row in Galatians to describe the perversion of the gospel he is preaching: "But even if we, or an angel from heaven, should preach to you a gospel contrary to (*para*) that which we preached to you, let him be accursed. As we have said before, so now I say again, If any one is preaching to you a gospel contrary to (*para*) that which you received, let him be accursed." (1:8-9)

1 Timothy: Chapter 6

I desire then that in every place the men should pray, lifting holy hands without anger or quarreling (*dialogismou*) ... (2:8)

Deacons likewise must be serious, not double-tongued (*dilogous*), not addicted to much wine, not greedy for gain ... (3:8)

Now the Spirit expressly says that in later times some will depart from the faith by giving heed to deceitful spirits and doctrines of demons, through the pretensions of liars (*psevdologōn*) whose consciences are seared ... (4:1-2)

If any one teaches otherwise and does not agree with the sound words of our Lord Jesus Christ and the teaching which accords with godliness, he is puffed up with conceit, he knows nothing; he has a morbid craving for controversy and for disputes about words (*logomakhias*), which produce envy, dissension, slander, base suspicions ... (6:3-4)

Unfortunately and to our detriment, the development of classical theology in all its different trends and "traditions" more often than not fell precisely in—and is still captive to—this trap of beguiling speech (*pithanologia*), foul talk (*aiskhrologian*), vain discussion (*mataiologian*), quarreling (*dialogismou*), disputes about words (*logomakhias*), and, worst of all, endless genealogies (*genealogiais*) of the names of those who supposedly upheld from generation to generation the so-called "living tradition," in overt contravention of the caveat at the start of Psalm 78: "Give ear, O my people, to my teaching; incline your ears to the words of my mouth!" Although scripture is utterly concerned with God's will, theology has made of it a complicated treatise *about* (the mystery of) God and his Christ, so much so that by the time the common believers are able to fathom it, they are without enough energy and time to fulfill the Lord's command to care for any and all needy brethren "for whom Christ died" (1 Cor 8:11b).

2 Timothy

Chapter 1

Vv. 1-18 ¹Παῦλος ἀπόστολος Χριστοῦ Ἰησοῦ διὰ θελήματος θεοῦ κατ᾽ ἐπαγγελίαν ζωῆς τῆς ἐν Χριστῷ Ἰησοῦ ²Τιμοθέῳ ἀγαπητῷ τέκνῳ, χάρις ἔλεος εἰρήνη ἀπὸ θεοῦ πατρὸς καὶ Χριστοῦ Ἰησοῦ τοῦ κυρίου ἡμῶν. ³Χάριν ἔχω τῷ θεῷ, ᾧ λατρεύω ἀπὸ προγόνων ἐν καθαρᾷ συνειδήσει, ὡς ἀδιάλειπτον ἔχω τὴν περὶ σοῦ μνείαν ἐν ταῖς δεήσεσίν μου νυκτὸς καὶ ἡμέρας, ⁴ἐπιποθῶν σε ἰδεῖν, μεμνημένος σου τῶν δακρύων, ἵνα χαρᾶς πληρωθῶ, ⁵ὑπόμνησιν λαβὼν τῆς ἐν σοὶ ἀνυποκρίτου πίστεως, ἥτις ἐνῴκησεν πρῶτον ἐν τῇ μάμμῃ σου Λωΐδι καὶ τῇ μητρί σου Εὐνίκῃ, πέπεισμαι δὲ ὅτι καὶ ἐν σοί. ⁶Δι᾽ ἣν αἰτίαν ἀναμιμνῄσκω σε ἀναζωπυρεῖν τὸ χάρισμα τοῦ θεοῦ, ὅ ἐστιν ἐν σοὶ διὰ τῆς ἐπιθέσεως τῶν χειρῶν μου. ⁷οὐ γὰρ ἔδωκεν ἡμῖν ὁ θεὸς πνεῦμα δειλίας ἀλλὰ δυνάμεως καὶ ἀγάπης καὶ σωφρονισμοῦ. ⁸μὴ οὖν ἐπαισχυνθῇς τὸ μαρτύριον τοῦ κυρίου ἡμῶν μηδὲ ἐμὲ τὸν δέσμιον αὐτοῦ, ἀλλὰ συγκακοπάθησον τῷ εὐαγγελίῳ κατὰ δύναμιν θεοῦ, ⁹τοῦ σώσαντος ἡμᾶς καὶ καλέσαντος κλήσει ἁγίᾳ, οὐ κατὰ τὰ ἔργα ἡμῶν ἀλλὰ κατὰ ἰδίαν πρόθεσιν καὶ χάριν, τὴν δοθεῖσαν ἡμῖν ἐν Χριστῷ Ἰησοῦ πρὸ χρόνων αἰωνίων, ¹⁰φανερωθεῖσαν δὲ νῦν διὰ τῆς ἐπιφανείας τοῦ σωτῆρος ἡμῶν Χριστοῦ Ἰησοῦ, καταργήσαντος μὲν τὸν θάνατον φωτίσαντος δὲ ζωὴν καὶ ἀφθαρσίαν διὰ τοῦ εὐαγγελίου ¹¹εἰς ὃ ἐτέθην ἐγὼ κῆρυξ καὶ ἀπόστολος καὶ διδάσκαλος, ¹²δι᾽ ἣν αἰτίαν καὶ ταῦτα πάσχω· ἀλλ᾽ οὐκ ἐπαισχύνομαι, οἶδα γὰρ ᾧ πεπίστευκα καὶ πέπεισμαι ὅτι δυνατός ἐστιν τὴν παραθήκην μου φυλάξαι εἰς ἐκείνην τὴν ἡμέραν. ¹³Ὑποτύπωσιν ἔχε ὑγιαινόντων λόγων ὧν παρ᾽ ἐμοῦ ἤκουσας ἐν πίστει καὶ ἀγάπῃ τῇ ἐν Χριστῷ Ἰησοῦ· ¹⁴τὴν καλὴν παραθήκην φύλαξον διὰ πνεύματος ἁγίου τοῦ ἐνοικοῦντος ἐν ἡμῖν. ¹⁵Οἶδας τοῦτο, ὅτι ἀπεστράφησάν με πάντες οἱ ἐν τῇ Ἀσίᾳ, ὧν ἐστιν Φύγελος καὶ Ἑρμογένης. ¹⁶δῴη ἔλεος ὁ κύριος τῷ Ὀνησιφόρου οἴκῳ, ὅτι πολλάκις με ἀνέψυξεν καὶ τὴν ἅλυσίν μου οὐκ ἐπαισχύνθη, ¹⁷ἀλλὰ γενόμενος ἐν Ῥώμῃ σπουδαίως ἐζήτησέν με καὶ εὗρεν· ¹⁸δῴη αὐτῷ ὁ κύριος εὑρεῖν ἔλεος παρὰ κυρίου ἐν ἐκείνῃ τῇ ἡμέρᾳ. καὶ ὅσα ἐν Ἐφέσῳ διηκόνησεν, βέλτιον σὺ γινώσκεις.

¹*Paul, an apostle of Christ Jesus by the will of God according to the promise of the life which is in Christ Jesus, ²To Timothy, my beloved child: Grace, mercy, and peace from God the Father and Christ Jesus our Lord. ³I thank God whom I serve with a clear conscience, as did my fathers, when I remember you constantly in my prayers. ⁴As I remember your tears, I long night and day to see you, that I may be filled with joy. ⁵I am reminded of your sincere faith, a faith that dwelt first in your grandmother Lois and your mother Eunice and now, I am sure, dwells in you. ⁶Hence I remind you to rekindle the gift of God that is within you through the laying on of my hands; ⁷for God did not give us a spirit of timidity but a spirit of power and love and self-control. ⁸Do not be ashamed then of testifying to our Lord, nor of me his prisoner, but share in suffering for the gospel in the power of God, ⁹who saved us and called us with a holy calling, not in virtue of our works but in virtue of his own purpose and the grace which he gave us in Christ Jesus ages ago, ¹⁰and now has manifested through the appearing of our Savior Christ Jesus, who abolished death and brought life and immortality to light through the gospel. ¹¹For this gospel I was appointed a preacher and apostle and teacher, ¹²and therefore I suffer as I do. But I am not ashamed, for I know whom I have believed, and I am sure that he is able to guard until that Day what has been entrusted to me. ¹³Follow the pattern of the sound words which you have heard from me, in the faith and love which are in Christ Jesus; ¹⁴guard the truth that has been entrusted to you by the Holy Spirit who dwells within us. ¹⁵You are aware that all who are in Asia turned away from me, and among them Phygelus and Hermogenes. ¹⁶May the Lord grant mercy to the household of Onesiphorus, for he often refreshed me; he was not ashamed of my chains, ¹⁷but when he arrived in Rome he searched for me eagerly and found me—¹⁸may the Lord grant*

him to find mercy from the Lord on that Day—and you well know all the service he rendered at Ephesus.

If 1 Timothy was conceived as *the* "deposit" of *the* "gospel" which is valid for both the Gentiles and the Jews,[1] then the question that comes to mind when dealing with 2 Timothy is what else could the author possibly add in a second letter to the same person without repeating himself. In fact, had Paul written 2 Timothy 4:6-8 toward the end of 1 Timothy, no one would have thought a second letter necessary, let alone forthcoming:

> For I am already on the point of being sacrificed; the time of my departure has come. I have fought the good fight, I have finished the race, I have kept the faith. Henceforth there is laid up for me the crown of righteousness, which the Lord, the righteous judge, will award to me on that Day, and not only to me but also to all who have loved his appearing. (2 Tim 4:6-8)

The most plausible answer is that this kind of repetition is a literary device inherent to scripture. The prototype for such pattern is found in the Pentateuch. It is evident in the way Deuteronomy re-visits the Mosaic Law of Exodus and Leviticus at the end of the journey through the wilderness that is described in Numbers. While Exodus and Leviticus were specifically handed to the scriptural Israel assumedly for the forty years when they were on their own in the wilderness, the iteration of the Law in Deuteronomy was issued to the next generation that was about to enter the earth of promise where they would reside among the nations who, in turn, will be required to abide by its statutes:

> At that time the Lord said to Joshua, "Make flint knives and circumcise the people of Israel again the second time." So Joshua made flint knives, and circumcised the people of Israel at Gibeath-haaraloth. And this is the reason why Joshua circumcised them: all

---

[1] See earlier my comments on the Gentile names Hymenaeus and Alexander in 1 Tim 1:20.

the males of the people who came out of Egypt, all the men of war, had died on the way in the wilderness after they had come out of Egypt. Though all the people who came out had been circumcised, yet all the people that were born on the way in the wilderness after they had come out of Egypt had not been circumcised. For the people of Israel walked forty years in the wilderness, till all the nation, the men of war that came forth out of Egypt, perished, because they did not hearken to the voice of the Lord; to them the Lord swore that he would not let them see the land which the Lord had sworn to their fathers to give us, a land flowing with milk and honey. So it was their children, whom he raised up in their stead, that Joshua circumcised; for they were uncircumcised, because they had not been circumcised on the way. (Josh 5:2-7)

Then Joshua built an altar in Mount Ebal to the Lord, the God of Israel, as Moses the servant of the Lord had commanded the people of Israel, as it is written in the book of the law of Moses, "an altar of unhewn stones, upon which no man has lifted an iron tool";[2] and they offered on it burnt offerings to the Lord, and sacrificed peace offerings. And there, in the presence of the people of Israel, he wrote upon the stones a copy of the law of Moses, which he had written. And all Israel, sojourner as well as homeborn, with their elders and officers and their judges, stood on opposite sides of the ark before the Levitical priests who carried the ark of the covenant of the Lord, half of them in front of Mount Gerizim and half of them in front of Mount Ebal, as Moses the servant of the Lord had commanded at the first, that they should bless the people of Israel.[3] And afterward he read all the words of the law, the blessing and the curse, according to all that is written in the book of the law. There was not a word of all that Moses commanded which Joshua did not read

---

[2] See Deut 27:4-6a: "And when you have passed over the Jordan, you shall set up these stones, concerning which I command you this day, on Mount Ebal, and you shall plaster them with plaster. And there you shall build an altar to the Lord your God, an altar of stones; you shall lift up no iron tool upon them. You shall build an altar to the Lord your God of unhewn stones."
[3] See Deut 11:29: "And when the Lord your God brings you into the land which you are entering to take possession of it, you shall set the blessing on Mount Gerizim and the curse on Mount Ebal."

before all the assembly of Israel, and the women, and the little ones, and the sojourners who lived among them. (8:30-35)

The same scenario occurs in the Pastoral Letters, and follows the pattern "first the Jew, but also the Gentile," which is underscored by Paul (Rom 1:16; 2:9, 10). Not only does 2 Timothy pick up where 1 Timothy left off, but at the end it is also filled with a long series of names of Gentile persons who, at least initially, endorsed the gospel. The mention of such names has been prepared for through the reference to Hymenaeus and Alexander at the beginning of 1 Timothy (1:20). These clearly Gentile names are mentioned again in 2 Timothy 2:17 (Among them are Hymenaeus and Philetus) and 4:14 (Alexander the coppersmith did me great harm; the Lord will requite him for his deeds). The link between the two epistles is established with the intent that they be read in tandem. The continuation of 1 Timothy 6 in 2 Timothy 1 can be presumed from the use of the noun *parathēkē* (deposit) that occurs only in 1 Timothy 6:20 and 2 Timothy 1:12, 14, to wit, in the phrase "guard (*phylax*—) the deposit." What seals the intentionality of the matter is that in the original, after the first two references to merely "the deposit" (*tēn parathēkēn*), the third time it is mentioned the deposit is qualified as "good" (*kalēn*), which is another adjective that is a staple of the Pastoral Letters:[4] "Now we know that the law is good, if any one uses it lawfully" (1 Tim 1:8). The goodness of the "deposit" of the gospel teaching stems from the goodness of the divine law embedded in scripture. Paul taught in Romans that he was "called to be an apostle, set apart for the gospel of God which he promised beforehand through his prophets in the holy scriptures" (1:1-2); "So the law is holy, and the commandment is holy and just and good (*agathē* [5])." (7:12) The last instance of "good," found in

---

[4] No less than 29 times over 13 chapters.
[5] The Greek adjectives *kalēn* and *agathē* are practically equivalent in meaning as is evident from what Paul writes further in Rom 7: "If then I do that which I would not, I consent unto the law that *it is* good (*kalos*). Now then it is no more I that do it, but

conjunction with the Pauline gospel of the love for the needy neighbor, brackets the Pastoral literature: "And let our people learn to apply themselves to good deeds, so as to help cases of urgent need, and not to be unfruitful." (Tit 3:14) This, in turn, harks back to Romans: "Owe no one anything, except to love one another; for he who loves his neighbor has fulfilled the law. The commandments, 'You shall not commit adultery, You shall not kill, You shall not steal, You shall not covet,' and any other commandment, are summed up in this sentence, 'You shall love your neighbor as yourself.' Love does no wrong to a neighbor; therefore love is the fulfilling of the law." (13:8-10)

This same concern is equally detectable in the unique way Paul introduces himself in conjunction with his apostolic activity: "For this gospel I was appointed a preacher (*kēryx*) and apostle (*apostolos*) and teacher (*didaskalos*)." (2 Tim 1:11) This statement is a reprise of what he wrote earlier in 1 Timothy: "For this I was appointed a preacher and apostle (I am telling the truth, I am not lying), *a teacher of the Gentiles* in faith and truth." (2:7) The reference to himself as "teacher," which is encountered nowhere else in the New Testament, is made in view of a Jew communicating the message *of the Law* to the Gentiles, as is clear from the only other occurrence of "teacher" (in the singular) in the Pauline corpus:

> But if you call yourself a Jew and rely upon the law and boast of your relation to God and know his will and approve what is excellent, because you are instructed in the law, and if you are sure that you are a guide to the blind, a light to those who are in

---

sin that dwelleth in me. For I know that in me (that is, in my flesh,) dwelleth no good thing (*agathon*): for to will is present with me; but *how* to perform that which is good (*kalon*) I find not. For the good (*agathon*) that I would I do not: but the evil which I would not, that I do." (vv.16-19 KJV)

darkness, a corrector of the foolish, *a teacher of children*,⁶ having in the law the embodiment of knowledge and truth—you then who *teach* others, will you not *teach* yourself? While you preach (*kēryssōn*; from the same root as *kēryx*) against stealing, do you steal? (Rom 2:17-21)

In presenting himself as a teacher, Paul is putting Timothy, who is not an apostle, on par with himself, in order to pressure him to continue on the path initiated by the apostle. At the end of the letter Paul will charge Timothy with these words: "preach (*kēryxon*; from the same root as *kēryx*) the word (of the Pauline gospel; *ton logon*), be urgent in season and out of season, convince, rebuke, and exhort, be unfailing in patience and in teaching." (2 Tim 4:2) That Timothy is Paul's primary and plenipotentiary trustee in the matter of leading the post-apostolic generation of believers is reflected in the phrase "my beloved (*agapētō*) child (*teknō*)" (2 Tim 1:2). The only other instance where Timothy is introduced thus is 1 Corinthians 4 where he is spoken of as "my beloved (*agapētō*) and faithful (*piston*) child (*teknon*) in the Lord, to *remind you* of my ways in Christ, *as I teach them everywhere in every church*" (v.17). Earlier in the passage the addressees were referred to as "my [Paul's] beloved (*agapēta*) children (*tekna*)" (v.14).

Paul's handling of Timothy parallels the Old Testament's handling of Joshua in relation to Moses. Joshua "appears" for the first time in scripture in Exodus 17 (vv.9-14), just in time to witness the first promulgation of the divine statutes (Ex 20-23). His special status as a rising star can be seen during the incident of the golden calf and the re-issuance of the Law (Ex 32-34):

---

⁶ It is obviously the Gentiles, the non-Jews, who are "blind, (being) in darkness, foolish, and children" since they are not privy to the Law. Notice the closeness between Romans and 2 Timothy in that both refer to the Law, respectively the gospel, as bringing light into darkness: "a light (*phōs*) to those who are in darkness" (Rom 2:19) and "[Christ] who abolished death and *brought* life and immortality *to light* (*phōtisantos*; enlightened) through the gospel" (2 Tim 1:10).

"When Joshua heard the noise of the people as they shouted, he said to Moses, 'There is a noise of war in the camp'" (32:17); "Thus the Lord used to speak to Moses face to face, as a man speaks to his friend. When Moses turned again into the camp, his servant Joshua the son of Nun, a young man, did not depart from the tent." (33:11) His position as the successor of Moses is sealed when he is commissioned to lead the people (Num 27:18-23), in view of Moses' dismissal before the entrance into the earth of the promise (Deut 1:37-38):

> And the Lord commissioned Joshua the son of Nun and said, "Be strong and of good courage; for you shall bring the children of Israel into the land which I swore to give them: I will be with you." (Deut 31:23)

> After the death of Moses the servant of the Lord, the Lord said to Joshua the son of Nun, Moses' minister, "Moses my servant is dead; now therefore arise, go over this Jordan, you and all this people, into the land which I am giving to them, to the people of Israel. Every place that the sole of your foot will tread upon I have given to you, as I promised to Moses. From the wilderness and this Lebanon as far as the great river, the river Euphrates, all the land of the Hittites to the Great Sea toward the going down of the sun shall be your territory. No man shall be able to stand before you all the days of your life; as I was with Moses, so I will be with you; I will not fail you or forsake you. Be strong and of good courage; for you shall cause this people to inherit the land which I swore to their fathers to give them. Only be strong and very courageous, being careful to do according to all the law which Moses my servant commanded you; turn not from it to the right hand or to the left, that you may have good success wherever you go. This book of the law shall not depart out of your mouth, but you shall meditate on it day and night, that you may be careful to do according to all that is written in it; for then you shall make your way prosperous, and then you shall have good success. Have I not commanded you? Be strong and of good courage; be not frightened, neither be dismayed; for the Lord your God is with you wherever you go." (Josh 1:1-9)

At the end of his life, Joshua, who was merely the minister of Moses, was granted the same title of "servant of the Lord" (Josh 24:29) that was reserved for Moses throughout the book (1:13, 15; 8:31, 33; 9:24; 11:12, 15; 12:6; 13:8; 14:7; 18:7; 22:2, 4, 5). Yet, upon his death (Judg 2:6-10), we hear:

> the people of Israel did what was evil in the sight of the Lord and served the Baals; and they forsook the Lord, the God of their fathers, who had brought them out of the land of Egypt; they went after other gods, from among the gods of the peoples who were round about them, and bowed down to them; and they provoked the Lord to anger. They forsook the Lord, and served the Baals and the Ashtaroth. So the anger of the Lord was kindled against Israel, and he gave them over to plunderers, who plundered them; and he sold them into the power of their enemies round about, so that they could no longer withstand their enemies. Whenever they marched out, the hand of the Lord was against them for evil, as the Lord had warned, and as the Lord had sworn to them; and they were in sore straits. (vv.11-15)

This obstinate recalcitrance will persist until God exiles the people from the earth of his promise (2 Kg 24-25). His promise to their descendants is that he will bring them, together with the nations, into his heavenly Zion (Is 66:18-21).

It is this scriptural teaching that lies behind the unexpected introduction in 2 Timothy, unique in the Pauline corpus: "Paul, an apostle of Christ Jesus by the will of God according to (in view of) *the promise of the life* which is in Christ Jesus" (1:1). Its understanding becomes clear when examined against the previous and only other reference to "promise" in the Pastoral Letters. The statement "The saying (*ho logos*; the word)[7] is sure (*pistos*) and

---

[7] This is the "word" of the Pauline gospel, as is evident from Acts and Paul's letters. See especially its similar use in 2 Cor: "As surely as God is faithful (*pistos*), our word (*logos*) to you has not been Yes and No. For the Son of God, Jesus Christ, whom we preached among you, Silvanus and Timothy and I, was not Yes and No; but in him it is always Yes." (1:18-19)

worthy of full acceptance, that Christ Jesus came into the world to save sinners" (1 Tim 1:15) is expanded later into "Have nothing to do with godless and silly myths. Train yourself in godliness; for while bodily training is of some value, godliness is of value in every way, as it holds *promise* for the present life and also *for the life to come*. The saying is sure and worthy of full acceptance. For to this end we toil and strive, because we have our hope set on the living God, who is the Savior of all men, especially of those who believe." (4:7-10) The first epistle underscored that the gospel teaching Paul preached was anchored in the Old Testament scripture (1 Tim 4:13) entrusted to the Jews (Rom 3:1). In the next epistle (2 Tim), Paul writes to Timothy, the bishop of the Pauline headquarters in Ephesus, which is the capital of the province Asia and home of the famous "temple of the great goddess Artemis" (Acts 19:27, 35), that the same gospel teaching is to be shared with the Gentiles.[8] They are invited to realize that the promise of life still lies ahead lest, after the deaths of Paul and Timothy, they end in permanent exile, as did the scriptural Israel after the death of Moses and Joshua. Being the "repeated" apostolic word, 2 Timothy sounds like a final testament for the ages:

> For I am already on the point of being sacrificed; the time of my departure has come. I have fought the good fight, I have finished the race, I have kept the faith. Henceforth there is laid up for me the crown of righteousness, which the Lord, the righteous judge, will award to me on that Day, and not only to me but also to all who have loved his appearing. (2 Tim 4:6-8)

The seriousness of the matter can be seen in that even after his death, Paul is not exempt from waiting for "that Day." "Holding that the resurrection is past already" amounts to "swerving from the truth" and is "godless chatter, leading people into more and more ungodliness" and "talk that eats its way like gangrene" and "upsets the faith" (2:16-18). Notice that it is Hymenaeus and

---

[8] A similar approach is found in 1 John and 2 John, see *NTI₃* 175-6.

Philetus who promulgate such teaching. So the message is, "Gentiles, beware; you are not exempt from forgetting the teaching of Paul and Timothy, just as the generations that arose after the deaths of Moses and Joshua were not exempt from their teaching."

That the Gentiles under Timothy's care are bound by the scriptures entrusted to the Jews is underlined in an interesting feature of 2 Timothy 1. In thanking God while remembering his addressee in his prayer Paul qualifies God as "whom I serve from *my* forefathers with pure conscience" (v.3).[9] The original can be rendered more accurately "I thank God, whom I serve [as I learned] from (*apo*) *my* forefathers with pure conscience," which makes much more sense when taken in conjunction with what we hear elsewhere:

> I am a Jew, born at Tarsus in Cilicia, but brought up in this city at the feet of Gamaliel, educated according to the strict manner of the law of our fathers, being zealous for God as you all are this day. I persecuted this Way to the death, binding and delivering to prison both men and women. (Acts 22:3-4)

> For you have heard of my former life in Judaism, how I persecuted the church of God violently and tried to destroy it; and I advanced in Judaism beyond many of my own age among my people, so extremely zealous was I for the traditions of my fathers. (Gal 1:13-14)

The value of scripture is further validated by the other example of a Jew who, like Paul, was "from childhood acquainted with the sacred writings which are able to instruct for salvation through faith in Christ Jesus" (2 Tim 3:15). Timothy is said to have

---

[9] I am following here KJV that is closer to the original than RSV, which reads "I thank God whom I serve with a clear conscience, *as did my fathers*, when I remember you constantly in my prayers."

learned from his grandmother and mother (1:5).[10] Moreover, the value of such instruction in the Law is enhanced by the two names the author chose to give them: *Lōis*[11] (Lois) means "advantageous, good" and *Evnikē* (Eunice) means "honorable or definitive victory." Consequently, the message to the hearers is that the real advantage of being brought up in the Law is the ultimate success promised in that same Law should one follow it. The sound *nikē* (victory) would have struck a chord in the ears of the Gentile Hellenes, heirs of Alexander of Macedon, and more so, in the ears of the Gentile Romans, heirs of Augustus Caesar who won his decisive victory in Philippi, the city established by Alexander's father, Philip II of Macedon. This is the message of the Book of Daniel that presages that the Kingdom of God will supersede all other earthly kingdoms.

Given that this letter sounds like Paul's final testament (2 Tim 4:6-8) one would expect to find in it and in 1 Timothy, its companion letter, echoes of the Pauline literature. Since Timothy, Paul's heir, is the bishop of Ephesus, one would expect a distinct echo of Ephesians, especially in 2 Timothy, and this is precisely what one finds in the first two chapters of this letter. To be sure, "sincere *anypokritou* faith" (2 Tim 1:5) is a clear reference to Galatians 2:13 (And with him the rest of the Jews acted insincerely, so that even Barnabas was carried away by their insincerity [*hypokrisei*]),[12] "bringing life and immortality to light" (2 Tim 1:10) brings to mind the lengthy discussions of Romans 6 and 1 Cor 15, and even "share in suffering for the gospel in the power of God" (2 Tim 1:8) recalls "and if children, then heirs, heirs of God and fellow heirs with Christ, provided we suffer with him in order that we may also be glorified with him" (Rom 8:17).

---

[10] In Acts Timothy is introduced as "the son of a Jewish woman who was a believer" (16:1), which was the reason behind Paul's circumcising him (v.3).

[11] *Lōis* becomes *Lōidi* in the dative case.

[12] See earlier my comments on 1 Tim 1:5 (sincere [*anypokritou*] faith) and 4:2 (the pretensions [*hypokrisei*] of liars).

However, 2 Timothy 1:8-12a is replete with the vocabulary as well as the thought pattern encountered in Ephesians 1-4:

> Do not be ashamed then of testifying to our Lord, nor of me his prisoner (*desmios*; chained, in chains), but share in suffering for the *gospel* in the power of God, who saved us and *called us with a holy calling, not in virtue of our works but in virtue of his own purpose and the grace which he gave us in Christ Jesus ages ago* (*pro khronōn aiōniōn*; before many ages), and now has manifested through the appearing of our Savior Christ Jesus, who abolished death and brought life and immortality to light through the gospel. For this gospel I was appointed a preacher and apostle and teacher, and therefore I suffer as I do. But I am not ashamed, for I know whom I have believed, and I am sure that he is able to guard until that Day what has been entrusted to me. Follow the pattern of the sound words which you have heard from me, in the faith and love which are in Christ Jesus; guard the truth that has been entrusted to you by the Holy Spirit who dwells within us. (2 Tim 1:8-14)

> Blessed be the God and Father of our Lord Jesus Christ, who has blessed us in Christ with every spiritual blessing in the heavenly places, even as he chose us in him before the foundation of the world, that we should be holy and blameless before him. He destined us in love to be his sons through Jesus Christ, according to the purpose of his will, to the praise of his glorious grace which he freely bestowed on us in the Beloved. In him we have redemption through his blood, the forgiveness of our trespasses, according to the riches of his grace which he lavished upon us. For he has made known to us in all wisdom and insight the mystery of his will, according to his purpose which he set forth in Christ as a plan for the fulness of time, to unite all things in him, things in heaven and things on earth. In him, according to the purpose of him who accomplishes all things according to the counsel of his will, we who first hoped in Christ have been destined and appointed to live for the praise of his glory. In him you also, who have heard the word of truth, the gospel of your salvation, and have believed in him, were sealed with the promised Holy Spirit, which is the guarantee of our

inheritance until we acquire possession of it, to the praise of his glory. (Eph 1:3-14)

For by grace you have been saved through faith; and this is not your own doing, it is the gift of God— not because of works, lest any man should boast. For we are his workmanship, created in Christ Jesus for good works, which God prepared beforehand, that we should walk in them. (2:8-10)

For this reason I, Paul, a prisoner for Christ Jesus on behalf of you Gentiles ... that is, how the Gentiles are fellow heirs, members of the same body, and partakers of the promise in Christ Jesus through the gospel. Of this gospel I was made a minister according to the gift of God's grace which was given me by the working of his power ... So I ask you not to lose heart over what I am suffering for you, which is your glory. (3:1, 6-7, 13)

I therefore, a prisoner for the Lord, beg you to lead a life worthy of the calling to which you have been called, with all lowliness and meekness, with patience, forbearing one another in love, eager to maintain the unity of the Spirit in the bond of peace. There is one body and one Spirit, just as you were called to the one hope that belongs to your call. (4:1-4)

As Paul taught in Romans 9-11, although God has expressed his mercy toward the Gentiles by sharing his law with them, they are not to take matters for granted by assuming that they would fare better than the scriptural Israel. This is precisely the function of the unexpected ominous verse, "You are aware that *all who are in Asia turned away from me*, and among them Phygelus and Hermogenes" (2 Tim 1:15). In order to understand that these two names function as representations of wrong attitudes, one should contrast them with the behavior of Onesiphorus to whom no less than three verses are dedicated. The correspondence of the names Onesiphorus and Onesimus (Col 4:9; Philem 10) parallel that between Epaphroditus (Phil 2:25; 4:18) and Epaphras (Col 4:12;

Philem 23). Both Onesiphorus and Onesimos mean "useful."[13] More importantly, they are described in the same terms:

> Do not be ashamed then of testifying to our Lord, nor of me his prisoner (*desmios*), but share in suffering *for the gospel* in the power of God ... May the Lord grant mercy to the household of Onesiphorus, for he often refreshed me; he was not ashamed of *my chains*, but when he arrived in Rome he searched for me eagerly and found me—may the Lord grant him to find mercy from the Lord on that Day—and you well know all *the service he rendered* (*diēkonēsen*) at Ephesus. (2 Tim 1:8, 16-18)

> Accordingly, though I am bold enough in Christ to command you to do what is required, yet for love's sake I prefer to appeal to you— I, Paul, an ambassador and now a prisoner (*desmios*; chained) also for Christ Jesus—I appeal to you for my child, Onesimus, whose father I have become in my imprisonment (*en tois desmois*; in the chains) ... I would have been glad to keep him with me, in order that he might serve (*diakonei*) me on your behalf during my imprisonment (*en tois desmois*; in the chains) *for the gospel*. (Philem 1:8-10, 13)

In contrast with the faithful Onesiphorus, the pair Phygelus and Hermogenes should be taken as a combination that yields negative results, in the same vein as Hymenaeus and Alexander (1 Tim 1:20). *Phygelos* is from the root *phygē* that means "fleeing, getting away" and thus "desertion," which fully reflects the verb "turned away" as is evident from the parallel statement at the end of the letter: "At my first defense no one took my part; all deserted me. May it not be charged against them!" (2 Tim 4:16) In and of itself Hermogenes, like Hymenaeus, would carry a positive connotation since its meaning is "progeny of Hermes," that is, "messenger of God's will." However, contrary to Onesiphorus who stuck with

---

[13] See my comments in *C-Col* 119.

Paul, Hermogenes decided to join Phygelus in deserting Paul. In so doing, Hermogenes betrayed his calling just as Hymenaeus did.

Chapter 2

Vv. 1-26 *¹Σὺ οὖν, τέκνον μου, ἐνδυναμοῦ ἐν τῇ χάριτι τῇ ἐν Χριστῷ Ἰησοῦ, ² καὶ ἃ ἤκουσας παρ' ἐμοῦ διὰ πολλῶν μαρτύρων, ταῦτα παράθου πιστοῖς ἀνθρώποις, οἵτινες ἱκανοὶ ἔσονται καὶ ἑτέρους διδάξαι. ³ συγκακοπάθησον ὡς καλὸς στρατιώτης Χριστοῦ Ἰησοῦ. ⁴ οὐδεὶς στρατευόμενος ἐμπλέκεται ταῖς τοῦ βίου πραγματείαις, ἵνα τῷ στρατολογήσαντι ἀρέσῃ· ⁵ ἐὰν δὲ καὶ ἀθλῇ τις, οὐ στεφανοῦται ἐὰν μὴ νομίμως ἀθλήσῃ· ⁶ τὸν κοπιῶντα γεωργὸν δεῖ πρῶτον τῶν καρπῶν μεταλαμβάνειν. ⁷ νόει ὃ λέγω· δώσει γάρ σοι ὁ κύριος σύνεσιν ἐν πᾶσιν.⁸ Μνημόνευε Ἰησοῦν Χριστὸν ἐγηγερμένον ἐκ νεκρῶν, ἐκ σπέρματος Δαυίδ, κατὰ τὸ εὐαγγέλιόν μου· ⁹ ἐν ᾧ κακοπαθῶ μέχρι δεσμῶν ὡς κακοῦργος. ἀλλὰ ὁ λόγος τοῦ θεοῦ οὐ δέδεται· ¹⁰ διὰ τοῦτο πάντα ὑπομένω διὰ τοὺς ἐκλεκτούς, ἵνα καὶ αὐτοὶ σωτηρίας τύχωσιν τῆς ἐν Χριστῷ Ἰησοῦ μετὰ δόξης αἰωνίου. ¹¹ πιστὸς ὁ λόγος· εἰ γὰρ συναπεθάνομεν, καὶ συζήσομεν· ¹² εἰ ὑπομένομεν, καὶ συμβασιλεύσομεν· εἰ ἀρνησόμεθα, κἀκεῖνος ἀρνήσεται ἡμᾶς· ¹³ εἰ ἀπιστοῦμεν, ἐκεῖνος πιστὸς μένει· ἀρνήσασθαι ἑαυτὸν οὐ δύναται. ¹⁴ Ταῦτα ὑπομίμνῃσκε, διαμαρτυρόμενος ἐνώπιον τοῦ κυρίου, μὴ λογομαχεῖν, ἐπ' οὐδὲν χρήσιμον, ἐπὶ καταστροφῇ τῶν ἀκουόντων. ¹⁵ σπούδασον σεαυτὸν δόκιμον παραστῆσαι τῷ θεῷ, ἐργάτην ἀνεπαίσχυντον, ὀρθοτομοῦντα τὸν λόγον τῆς ἀληθείας. ¹⁶ τὰς δὲ βεβήλους κενοφωνίας περιΐστασο· ἐπὶ πλεῖον γὰρ προκόψουσιν ἀσεβείας, ¹⁷ καὶ ὁ λόγος αὐτῶν ὡς γάγγραινα νομὴν ἕξει· ὧν ἐστιν Ὑμέναιος καὶ Φίλητος, ¹⁸ οἵτινες περὶ τὴν ἀλήθειαν ἠστόχησαν, λέγοντες ἀνάστασιν ἤδη γεγονέναι, καὶ ἀνατρέπουσιν τὴν τινων πίστιν. ¹⁹ ὁ μέντοι στερεὸς θεμέλιος τοῦ θεοῦ ἕστηκεν, ἔχων τὴν σφραγῖδα ταύτην· Ἔγνω κύριος τοὺς ὄντας αὐτοῦ, καί· Ἀποστήτω ἀπὸ ἀδικίας πᾶς ὁ ὀνομάζων τὸ ὄνομα κυρίου. ²⁰ Ἐν μεγάλῃ δὲ οἰκίᾳ οὐκ ἔστιν μόνον σκεύη χρυσᾶ καὶ ἀργυρᾶ ἀλλὰ καὶ ξύλινα καὶ ὀστράκινα, καὶ ἃ μὲν εἰς τιμὴν ἃ δὲ εἰς ἀτιμίαν· ²¹ ἐὰν οὖν τις ἐκκαθάρῃ ἑαυτὸν ἀπὸ τούτων, ἔσται σκεῦος εἰς τιμήν, ἡγιασμένον, εὔχρηστον τῷ δεσπότῃ, εἰς πᾶν ἔργον ἀγαθὸν ἡτοιμασμένον. ²² τὰς δὲ* νεωτερικὰς ἐπιθυμίας φεῦγε, δίωκε δὲ δικαιοσύνην, πίστιν, ἀγάπην, εἰρήνην μετὰ τῶν ἐπικαλουμένων τὸν κύριον ἐκ καθαρᾶς καρδίας. ²³ τὰς δὲ μωρὰς καὶ ἀπαιδεύτους ζητήσεις παραιτοῦ, εἰδὼς ὅτι γεννῶσι μάχας· ²⁴ δοῦλον δὲ κυρίου οὐ δεῖ μάχεσθαι, ἀλλὰ ἤπιον εἶναι πρὸς πάντας, διδακτικόν, ἀνεξίκακον, ²⁵ ἐν πραΰτητι παιδεύοντα τοὺς ἀντιδιατιθεμένους, μήποτε δώῃ αὐτοῖς ὁ θεὸς μετάνοιαν εἰς ἐπίγνωσιν ἀληθείας, ²⁶ καὶ ἀνανήψωσιν ἐκ τῆς τοῦ διαβόλου παγίδος, ἐζωγρημένοι ὑπ' αὐτοῦ εἰς τὸ ἐκείνου θέλημα.

¹*You then, my son, be strong in the grace that is in Christ Jesus,* ²*and what you have heard from me before many witnesses entrust to faithful men who will be able to teach others also.* ³*Share in suffering as a good soldier of Christ Jesus.* ⁴*No soldier on service gets entangled in civilian pursuits, since his aim is to satisfy the one who enlisted him.* ⁵*An athlete is not crowned unless he competes according to the rules.* ⁶*It is the hard-working farmer who ought to have the first share of the crops.* ⁷*Think over what I say, for the Lord will grant you understanding in everything.* ⁸*Remember Jesus Christ, risen from the dead, descended from David, as preached in my gospel,* ⁹*the gospel for which I am suffering and wearing fetters like a criminal. But the word of God is not fettered.* ¹⁰*Therefore I endure everything for the sake of the elect, that they also may obtain salvation in Christ Jesus with its eternal glory.* ¹¹*The saying is sure: If we have died with him, we shall also live with him;* ¹²*if we endure, we shall also reign with him; if we deny him, he also will deny us;* ¹³*if we are faithless, he remains faithful—for he cannot deny himself.* ¹⁴*Remind them of this, and charge them before the Lord*ᴱ *to avoid disputing about words which does no good, but only ruins the hearers.* ¹⁵*Do your best to present yourself to God as one approved, a workman who has no need to be ashamed, rightly handling the word of truth.* ¹⁶*Avoid such godless chatter for it will lead people into more and more ungodliness,* ¹⁷*and their talk will eat its way like gangrene. Among them are Hymenaeus and Philetus,* ¹⁸*who have*

swerved from the truth by holding that the resurrection is past already. They are upsetting the faith of some. ¹⁹But God's firm foundation stands, bearing this seal: "The Lord knows those who are his," and, "Let every one who names the name of the Lord depart from iniquity." ²⁰In a great house there are not only vessels of gold and silver but also of wood and earthenware, and some for noble use, some for ignoble. ²¹If any one purifies himself from what is ignoble, then he will be a vessel for noble use, consecrated and useful to the master of the house, ready for any good work. ²²So shun youthful passions and aim at righteousness, faith, love, and peace, along with those who call upon the Lord from a pure heart. ²³Have nothing to do with stupid, senseless controversies; you know that they breed quarrels. ²⁴And the Lord's servant must not be quarrelsome but kindly to every one, an apt teacher, forbearing, ²⁵correcting his opponents with gentleness. God may perhaps grant that they will repent and come to know the truth, ²⁶and they may escape from the snare of the devil, after being captured by him to do his will.

After having ensured that his gospel teaching expanded upon in 1 Timothy was bequeathed as the "deposit" (*parathēkē*), Paul's insists in 2 Timothy 2 that this deposit be preserved "as is" by the leaders who follow after Timothy.[1] Paul introduced his first letter as a charge he committed as the deposit (*paratithemai*) to "Timothy, my son" (1 Tim 1:18). In 2 Timothy he requests that Timothy proceed accordingly with his own followers: "You then, *my son*, be strong in the grace that is in Christ Jesus, and what you have heard from me before many witnesses entrust (*parathou*; imperative of the verb *paratithemai*)[2] to *faithful men who will be able to teach others also.*" (2 Tim 1:1-2) Consequently, this descending line of teachers is bound by Paul's teaching, since

---

[1] See my argument against "oral tradition" in the section "Tradition and Deposit" at the end of my comments on 1 Timothy 6.
[2] These are the only two instances of that verb in the Pastoral Letters.

Timothy is asked to hand down to his followers the "deposit" already inscribed in the Pastoral Letters and in the other Pauline letters to the churches throughout the Roman empire.

Paul resorts to two stratagems to ensure the success of this delicate mission. The first is to deftly eliminate any inherent superiority of Timothy *over* his followers due to his chronological precedence. He rephrases his request to Timothy in the previous chapter, "Do not be ashamed then of testifying to our Lord, nor of me his prisoner, but share in suffering (*synkakopathēson*) for the gospel in the power of God" (2 Tim 1:8) by calling him a soldier and challenging him to be a good one: "Share in suffering (*synkakopathēson*)[3] as a good soldier (*stratiōtēs*) of Christ Jesus." (2:3) For an attentive hearer of scripture this carries with it a somewhat "demeaning" resonance when compared with a previous and a subsequent occurrence of "soldier," especially since the three sole instances of "soldier" apply to a specific person in the New Testament. Earlier in Philippians 2:19-30,[4] although Timothy is presented as Paul's heir apparent in the loftiest possible terms, nevertheless, it is Epaphroditus, the second in line, who is deemed not only Paul's "fellow soldier" (*systratiōtēn*), but also his "fellow worker" (*synergon*), that is, on par with Timothy himself (1 Thess 3:2):

> I hope in the Lord Jesus to send Timothy to you soon, so that I may be cheered by news of you. I have no one like him, who will be genuinely anxious for your welfare. They all look after their own interests, not those of Jesus Christ. But Timothy's worth you know, how as a son with a father he has served with me in the gospel ... I have thought it necessary to send to you Epaphroditus my brother and fellow worker and fellow soldier, and your messenger and minister to my need, for he has been longing for you all, and has

---

[3] These are the only two instances of that verb in the entire New Testament.
[4] See my detailed comments on this passage in *C-Phil* 139-47.

been distressed because you heard that he was ill. (Phil 2:19-22, 25-26)

In the text of Philemon one hears of a similar honor bestowed upon an even lesser leader than Epaphroditus. Archippus, a member of the household of Philemon, is honored with the title of "fellow soldier" as are Timothy and Epaphroditus:

> Paul, a prisoner for Christ Jesus, and Timothy our brother, to Philemon our beloved fellow worker and Apphia our sister and Archippus our fellow soldier, and the church in your house (Philem 1-2)

Another stratagem used to ensure the success of his mission is to write the rest of the chapter in a way that is reminiscent of both 1 Timothy and the Pauline corpus in general so that Paul's gospel would be "heard" *as a deposit*. Below are transcriptions of 2 Timothy 2:5-26 with annotations of their sources:

> [5] An athlete is not crowned unless he competes according to the rules. (*1 Cor 9: 24-27*)

> [6] It is the hard-working farmer who ought to have the first share of the crops. (*1 Cor 9:7, 10*)

> [7] Think over what I say, for the Lord will grant you understanding in everything. [8] Remember Jesus Christ, risen from the dead, descended from David, as preached in my gospel, (*Rom 1:1-4*)

> [9] the gospel for which I am suffering (*kakopathō*) and wearing fetters (*desmōn*; chains, from the same root as *desmios* [prisoner, chained]) like a criminal. (*2 Tim 1:8; Captivity Epistles [Ephesians, Philippians, and Colossians] and Philemon*) But the word of God is not fettered. (*Acts passim*)

¹⁰ Therefore I endure everything for the sake of the elect, that they also may obtain salvation in Christ Jesus with its eternal glory. (*1 Cor 9:19-23*)

¹¹ The saying is sure (*1 Tim 1:15; 3:1; 4:9*): If we have died with him, we shall also live with him (*Rom 6:4-10*)

¹² if we endure, we shall also reign with him (*Rom 5:17*); if we deny him, he also will deny us;

¹³ if we are faithless, he remains faithful (*1 Cor 1:9; 10:13; 2 Cor 1:18; 2 Thess 3:3*)—for he cannot deny himself.

¹⁴ Remind them of this, and charge them before the Lord to avoid *disputing about words* which does no good, but only ruins the hearers. (*1 Tim 6:4*)

¹⁵ Do your best to present yourself to God as one approved, a workman (*ergatēn, laborer; 1 Tim 5:18*) who has no need to be ashamed, rightly handling the word of truth. (*Gal 2:5, 14; the truth of the gospel*)

¹⁶ Avoid such *godless chatter* (*1 Tim 6:20*) for it will lead people into more and more ungodliness (*asebeias*),[5]

¹⁷ and their talk will eat its way like gangrene. Among them are Hymenaeus and Philetus,

¹⁸ who have swerved from (*ēstokhēsan*) the truth[6] (*1 Tim 1:6; 6:21; Gal 5:7*) by holding that the resurrection is past already (*1 Cor 15; 2 Thess 2:1-12*). They are upsetting the faith of some.

¹⁹ But God's firm foundation[7] stands, bearing this seal: "The Lord knows those who are his," and, "Let every one who names the name of the Lord depart from iniquity."

---

[5] *asebeias* is the opposite of "godliness" (*evsebeia*) mentioned so often in 1 Timothy.
[6] "of the Pauline gospel" (v.15; Gal 2:5, 14).
[7] Rom 15:20; 1 Cor 3:10-12; Eph 2:20; 1 Tim 6:19.

²⁰ In a great house there are not only vessels of gold and silver but also of wood and earthenware, and some for noble use, some for ignoble. (*1 Cor 3:10-15*)

²¹ If any one purifies himself from what is ignoble, then he will be a *vessel* for noble use, consecrated and useful to the master of the house, ready for any good work. (*Rom 9:21*)

²² So shun youthful passions and aim at righteousness, faith, love, and peace, along with those who call upon the Lord from a pure heart. (*1 Tim 6:1-11*)

²³ Have nothing to do with stupid, senseless controversies (*1 Tim 6:4*); you know that they breed quarrels (*1 Tim 3:3; 6:4*).

²⁴ And the Lord's servant must not be quarrelsome but kindly to every one, an apt teacher, forbearing, *(1 Tim 3:2-3)*

²⁵ correcting his opponents with gentleness (*Gal 6:1-2*). God may perhaps grant that they will repent and come to know the truth,[8]

²⁶ and they may escape from the snare of the devil, after being captured by him to do his will. (*1 Cor 5:1-5*)

How would one account for the two names Hymenaeus and Philetus? The discussion of the previous instance of Hymenaeus (1 Tim 1:20) has shown that although the name appeared to be positive, it was distorted by the negative connotation of its companion Alexander.[9] The same applies to *Philētos* (Philetus), which is the only Greek personal name ending in *–tos* in the New Testament.[10] It is constructed from *philoteon* whose meaning is "to be loved; must be loved"[11] and thus "needful for love."

---

[8] "of the Pauline gospel" (v.15; Gal 2:5, 14).
[9] Pp. 45-46.
[10] *Klēmentos* (Phil 4:3) is a Grecized transliteration of the original Latin *Clemens* (Clement). See my comments in *C-Phil* 180.
[11] This is the connotation of the (adjectival) ending *–teon* after a verbal root. The unique such instance in the New Testament is found in Lk 5:38: "But new wine must be put (*blēteon* [must be thrown] from the verb *ballō* [throw]) into fresh wineskins."

Consequently, just as the positive connotation of marriage resulting in procreation and multiplication of the human race (Hymenaeus) was corrupted by a multiplication of subjugating power (Alexander), so also here marriage that entails love for a spouse and children (Hymenaeus) is corrupted by love of oneself. In other words, taken together, Hymenaeus and Philetus are representatives of those who distort the core of the Pauline gospel which is love for any needy other.

Chapter 3

Vv. 1-17 ¹ Τοῦτο δὲ γίνωσκε ὅτι ἐν ἐσχάταις ἡμέραις ἐνστήσονται καιροὶ χαλεποί· ² ἔσονται γὰρ οἱ ἄνθρωποι φίλαυτοι, φιλάργυροι, ἀλαζόνες, ὑπερήφανοι, βλάσφημοι, γονεῦσιν ἀπειθεῖς, ἀχάριστοι, ἀνόσιοι, ³ ἄστοργοι, ἄσπονδοι, διάβολοι, ἀκρατεῖς, ἀνήμεροι, ἀφιλάγαθοι, ⁴ προδόται, προπετεῖς, τετυφωμένοι, φιλήδονοι μᾶλλον ἢ φιλόθεοι, ⁵ ἔχοντες μόρφωσιν εὐσεβείας τὴν δὲ δύναμιν αὐτῆς ἠρνημένοι· καὶ τούτους ἀποτρέπου. ⁶ ἐκ τούτων γάρ εἰσιν οἱ ἐνδύνοντες εἰς τὰς οἰκίας καὶ αἰχμαλωτίζοντες γυναικάρια σεσωρευμένα ἁμαρτίαις, ἀγόμενα ἐπιθυμίαις ποικίλαις, ⁷ πάντοτε μανθάνοντα καὶ μηδέποτε εἰς ἐπίγνωσιν ἀληθείας ἐλθεῖν δυνάμενα. ⁸ ὃν τρόπον δὲ Ἰάννης καὶ Ἰαμβρῆς ἀντέστησαν Μωϋσεῖ, οὕτως καὶ οὗτοι ἀνθίστανται τῇ ἀληθείᾳ, ἄνθρωποι κατεφθαρμένοι τὸν νοῦν, ἀδόκιμοι περὶ τὴν πίστιν. ⁹ ἀλλ᾽ οὐ προκόψουσιν ἐπὶ πλεῖον, ἡ γὰρ ἄνοια αὐτῶν ἔκδηλος ἔσται πᾶσιν, ὡς καὶ ἡ ἐκείνων ἐγένετο. ¹⁰ Σὺ δὲ παρηκολούθησάς μου τῇ διδασκαλίᾳ, τῇ ἀγωγῇ, τῇ προθέσει, τῇ πίστει, τῇ μακροθυμίᾳ, τῇ ἀγάπῃ, τῇ ὑπομονῇ, ¹¹ τοῖς διωγμοῖς, τοῖς παθήμασιν, οἷά μοι ἐγένετο ἐν Ἀντιοχείᾳ, ἐν Ἰκονίῳ, ἐν Λύστροις, οἵους διωγμοὺς ὑπήνεγκα· καὶ ἐκ πάντων με ἐρρύσατο ὁ κύριος. ¹² καὶ πάντες δὲ οἱ θέλοντες ζῆν εὐσεβῶς ἐν Χριστῷ Ἰησοῦ διωχθήσονται· ¹³ πονηροὶ δὲ ἄνθρωποι καὶ γόητες προκόψουσιν ἐπὶ τὸ χεῖρον, πλανῶντες καὶ πλανώμενοι. ¹⁴ σὺ δὲ μένε ἐν οἷς ἔμαθες καὶ ἐπιστώθης, εἰδὼς παρὰ τίνων ἔμαθες, ¹⁵ καὶ ὅτι ἀπὸ βρέφους ἱερὰ γράμματα οἶδας, τὰ δυνάμενά σε σοφίσαι εἰς σωτηρίαν διὰ πίστεως τῆς ἐν Χριστῷ Ἰησοῦ· ¹⁶ πᾶσα γραφὴ θεόπνευστος καὶ ὠφέλιμος πρὸς διδασκαλίαν, πρὸς ἐλεγμόν, πρὸς ἐπανόρθωσιν, πρὸς παιδείαν τὴν ἐν δικαιοσύνῃ, ¹⁷ ἵνα ἄρτιος ᾖ ὁ τοῦ θεοῦ ἄνθρωπος, πρὸς πᾶν ἔργον ἀγαθὸν ἐξηρτισμένος.

¹*But understand this, that in the last days there will come times of stress.* ²*For men will be lovers of self, lovers of money, proud, arrogant, abusive, disobedient to their parents, ungrateful,*

unholy, ³inhuman, implacable, slanderers, profligates, fierce, haters of good, ⁴treacherous, reckless, swollen with conceit, lovers of pleasure rather than lovers of God, ⁵holding the form of religion but denying the power of it. Avoid such people. ⁶For among them are those who make their way into households and capture weak women, burdened with sins and swayed by various impulses, ⁷who will listen to anybody and can never arrive at a knowledge of the truth. ⁸As Jannes and Jambres opposed Moses, so these men also oppose the truth, men of corrupt mind and counterfeit faith; ⁹but they will not get very far, for their folly will be plain to all, as was that of those two men. ¹⁰Now you have observed my teaching, my conduct, my aim in life, my faith, my patience, my love, my steadfastness, ¹¹my persecutions, my sufferings, what befell me at Antioch, at Iconium, and at Lystra, what persecutions I endured; yet from them all the Lord rescued me. ¹²Indeed all who desire to live a godly life in Christ Jesus will be persecuted, ¹³while evil men and impostors will go on from bad to worse, deceivers and deceived. ¹⁴But as for you, continue in what you have learned and have firmly believed, knowing from whom you learned it ¹⁵and how from childhood you have been acquainted with the sacred writings which are able to instruct you for salvation through faith in Christ Jesus. ¹⁶All scripture is inspired by God and profitable for teaching, for reproof, for correction, and for training in righteousness, ¹⁷that the man of God may be complete, equipped for every good work.

Now that he has left his writings as a deposit (2 Tim 2), that is, as a written and thus unchangeable legacy for all upcoming generations, and in view of his final farewell (4:6-8), Paul conceives chapters 3 and 4 with the aim of canonizing the entire New Testament literature *as scripture*.[1] In order to accomplish this, he plays at different levels at the same time.

---

[1] He did that in Colossians 4:10-17. See *C-Col* 95-106.

First he reminds Timothy, and through him all hearers, that the end time is at hand (2 Tim 3:1), just as he has repeatedly done, especially in his letter to the Romans:

> Besides this you know what hour it is, how it is full time now for you to wake from sleep. For salvation is nearer to us now than when we first believed; the night is far gone, the day is at hand. Let us then cast off the works of darkness and put on the armor of light; let us conduct ourselves becomingly as in the day, not in reveling and drunkenness, not in debauchery and licentiousness, not in quarreling and jealousy. But put on the Lord Jesus Christ, and make no provision for the flesh, to gratify its desires (*epithymias*). (Rom 13:11-14)

The desires of the flesh, that is, of the human will, are in opposition to the will of God's spirit, the fruit of which is love in all its aspects:

> But I say, walk by the Spirit, and do not gratify the desires of the flesh ... Now the works of the flesh are plain: fornication, impurity, licentiousness, idolatry, sorcery, enmity, strife, jealousy, anger, selfishness, dissension, party spirit, envy, drunkenness, carousing, and the like. I warn you, as I warned you before, that those who do such things shall not inherit the kingdom of God. But the fruit of the Spirit is love, joy, peace, patience, kindness, goodness, faithfulness, gentleness, self-control ... And those who belong to Christ Jesus have crucified the flesh with its passions and desires (*epithymiais*). If we live by the Spirit, let us also walk by the Spirit. Let us have no self-conceit, no provoking of one another, no envy of one another. (Gal 5:16, 19-26)

In 2 Timothy 3 the long list of misdeeds is bracketed between love of self (v. 1) and love of God (v. 4). What is worthy of note is that the original for "love of self" is *philavtoi* (self-lovers), a unique instance in the New Testament, which corresponds to the equally unique *Philētos* (Philetus; 2:17), showed earlier to be the prototype of those who distort the Pauline gospel.

Following his lead in Galatians and Romans where love for the needy is presented as the fulfilment of the Law (Gal 5:13-15; Rom 13:8-10), Paul prefaces the mention of his teaching and behavior (2 Tim 3:10-11) with a reference to Moses and uses the same terms: "As (*hon tropon*; in the same way as) Jannes and Jambres *opposed* Moses, so these men *also* (*houtōs kai*) *oppose* the truth, men of corrupt mind and counterfeit faith; but they will not get very far, for their folly will be plain to all, as was that of those two men." (vv.8-9)[2] The result is that the hearers perceive that Paul is putting himself as well as his teaching on par with Moses and the Law. This is done in preparation for vv.14-15 where Timothy will be reminded that he is bound by both sources of teaching.

Paul then very skillfully brings into the picture the Book of Acts through an otherwise unnecessary reference to the triad Antioch, Iconium, and Lystra, a combination that occurs only in Acts (14:21). Other than in 2 Timothy, Iconium, and Lystra are found only in Acts (14:6, 18, 21; 16:1);[3] Antioch is found repeatedly only in Acts[4] with the exception of Galatians 2:11. Since the book of Acts is the companion volume of the Gospel of Luke, the subtle reference to Acts here functions as a stepping stone toward the inclusion, later in 2 Timothy 4:11, of Luke and Mark—and by extension their Gospels—into the New Testament scripture.[5] For the time being, however, Paul is making the point that the written "deposit" of both his letters and the Book of Acts that contain information regarding his behavior as well as his teaching (2 Tim 3:1-11) have equal standing (v.14) with "the sacred writings (of the Old Testament)" (v.15) so that "all scripture" (v.16) would be understood as encompassing both. This supposition is substantiated in that scripture's first function is "teaching" (*didaskalian*) which has just been introduced as "*my* teaching" in

---

[2] See the excursus at the chapter's end on these two names.
[3] Iconium in Acts 13:51; 14:1, 19, 21; 16:2; and Lystra in Acts 14:6, 8, 21; 16:1, 2.
[4] No less than 16 times.
[5] See my discussion of Col 4:10-17 in *C-Col* 95-106.

v.10: "Now you have observed *my* teaching, my conduct, my aim in life, my faith, my patience, my love, my steadfastness, my persecutions, my sufferings." (vv.10-11a)[6] Paul is putting his teaching in writing should he not have the opportunity to personally encounter Timothy before he dies: "I hope to come to you soon, but I am writing these instructions to you so that, if I am delayed, you may know how one ought to behave in the household of God, which is the church of the living God, the pillar and bulwark of the truth." (1 Tim 3:14-15) He previously used this stratagem, that is, writing due to his lack of assurance that he would have the opportunity to see his addressees, in the Captivity Epistles[7] while being "chained (toward his eventual demise)." We also see this stratagem in Romans:

> This is the reason why I have so often been hindered from coming to you. But now, since I no longer have any room for work in these regions, and since I have longed for many years to come to you, I hope to see you in passing as I go to Spain, and to be sped on my journey there by you, once I have enjoyed your company for a little. At present, however, I am going to Jerusalem with aid for the saints. For Macedonia and Achaia have been pleased to make some contribution for the poor among the saints at Jerusalem; they were pleased to do it, and indeed they are in debt to them, for if the Gentiles have come to share in their spiritual blessings, they ought also to be of service to them in material blessings. When therefore I have completed this, and have delivered to them what has been raised, I shall go on by way of you to Spain; and I know that when I come to you I shall come in the fulness of the blessing of Christ. I appeal to you, brethren, by our Lord Jesus Christ and by the love of the Spirit, to strive together with me in your prayers to God on my behalf, that I may be delivered from the unbelievers in Judea, and that my service for Jerusalem may be acceptable to the saints,

---

[6] In the original, the possessive "my" (*mou*) is not repeated but precedes the entire series of nouns so that, to the ear, the stress of the possessive falls on (Paul's) teaching.
[7] Ephesians, Philippians, Colossians, Philemon.

so that by God's will I may come to you with joy and be refreshed in your company. (Rom 15:22-32)

It bears repeating that neither the "teaching" nor the "knowledge" is a matter of mental "understanding" or "perception" which, in turn, can be communicated in a way that the hearer would mentally fathom what the teacher himself had mentally comprehended. Unfortunately, in classical theology "divine training" has become an exercise in mental debates, rather than in teaching that entails reproof, correction, and training in acting righteously with the aim of *doing* "every good work":

> All scripture is inspired by God and profitable for teaching, for reproof, for correction, and for training in righteousness, (*so*) *that* (*hina*) the man of God may be complete, equipped for every good work (*pan ergon agathon*). (2 Tim 3:16-17)

It is "all good work" that is expected of the recipients of the teaching:

> In a great house there are not only vessels of gold and silver but also of wood and earthenware, and some for noble use, some for ignoble. If any one purifies himself from what is ignoble, then he will be a vessel for noble use, consecrated and useful to the master of the house, ready for any (every) good work (*pan ergon agathon*). (2:20-21)

Jannes and Jambres

I have opted for an excursus on the use of Jannes and Jambres since the topic warrants some detail and an aside would have interrupted the flow of my argument. On the other hand and for the same reason, a footnote would have been too lengthy. Jannes seems to be part of the lore surrounding Pharaoh's magicians who challenged Moses and Aaron (Ex 7:10-12; 8:5-7), as is evident from his mention by Pliny the Elder (23-79 A.D.):

> There is another sect, also, of adepts in the magic art, who derive their origin from Moses, Jannes, and Lotapea, Jews by birth, but many thousand years posterior to Zoroaster: and as much more recent, again, is the branch of magic cultivated in Cyprus.[8]

However, even if this were the case, it does not explain why Paul would specifically reference Jannes (*Iannēs*), especially since he was evidently aware of the so many other opponents of Moses mentioned by name in scripture. The most plausible explanation would be that Jannes appears a part of a pair of names, the second of which, Jambres (*Iambrēs*), has been coined by Paul himself.[9] In 1 Maccabees one hears the following account of the only two instances of the root *Iambr*— used in conjunction with a personal name:

> Then all the friends of Judas assembled and said to Jonathan: "Since the death of your brother Judas there has been no one like him to go against our enemies and Bacchides,[10] and to deal with those of our nation who hate us. So now we have chosen you today to take his place as our ruler and leader, to fight our battle." And Jonathan at that time accepted the leadership and took the place of Judas his brother. When Bacchides learned of this, he tried to kill him. But Jonathan and Simon his brother and all who were with him heard of it, and they fled into the wilderness of Tekoa and camped by the

---

[8] Pliny the Elder, *Naturalis Historia* (Natural History), Book 30, Chapter 2.
[9] All occurrences of that name are found in Post New Testament writings.
[10] A general in the army of the Seleucid King Demetrius (1 Macc 8:1).

water of the pool of Asphar. Bacchides found this out on the sabbath day, and he with all his army crossed the Jordan. And Jonathan sent his brother as leader of the multitude and begged the Nabateans, who were his friends, for permission to store with them the great amount of baggage which they had. But the sons of Jambri (*Iambri*) from Medeba came out and seized John and all that he had, and departed with it. After these things it was reported to Jonathan and Simon his brother: "The sons of Jambri (*Iambri*) are celebrating a great wedding, and are conducting the bride, a daughter of one of the great nobles of Canaan, from Nadabath with a large escort." And they remembered the blood of John their brother, and went up and hid under cover of the mountain. They raised their eyes and looked, and saw a tumultuous procession with much baggage; and the bridegroom came out with his friends and his brothers to meet them with tambourines and musicians and many weapons. Then they rushed upon them from the ambush and began killing them. Many were wounded and fell, and the rest fled to the mountain; and they took all their goods. Thus the wedding was turned into mourning and the voice of their musicians into a funeral dirge. And when they had fully avenged the blood of their brother, they returned to the marshes of the Jordan. When Bacchides heard of this, he came with a large force on the sabbath day to the banks of the Jordan. (9:28-43)

So, to someone cognizant of scripture, *Iambrēs* brings to mind an outsider, a Gentile. If such is the case, then that name forms a Jew-Gentile pair with *Iannēs*, like *Iōannēs* (John) a rendering of the Hebrew Hananiah (*ḥananyah*) or Yohannan (*yoḥannan*) whose meaning is "the Lord is graceful, merciful."[11] Again, someone cognizant of scripture, will remember that Hananiah, the prophet of the Jerusalem temple, was the nemesis of Jeremiah, the prophet from Anathoth (Jer 28). Consequently, the pair Jannes and Jambres functions as all the other pairs of names in the Pastoral Letters, that is to show that the man of God is betrayed by insiders

---

[11] Notice how the traditional Jewish dealings with the pair Jannes and Jambres render sometimes the former as *yoḥanay*.

and outsiders alike. Just as Moses had to face enemies from within and without, so did Paul. His being the true apostle against all odds is no less than Moses' being the true prophet against all odds.

Chapter 4

Vv. 1-22 ¹Διαμαρτύρομαι ἐνώπιον τοῦ θεοῦ καὶ Χριστοῦ Ἰησοῦ, τοῦ μέλλοντος κρίνειν ζῶντας καὶ νεκρούς, καὶ τὴν ἐπιφάνειαν αὐτοῦ καὶ τὴν βασιλείαν αὐτοῦ· ² κήρυξον τὸν λόγον, ἐπίστηθι εὐκαίρως ἀκαίρως, ἔλεγξον, ἐπιτίμησον, παρακάλεσον, ἐν πάσῃ μακροθυμίᾳ καὶ διδαχῇ. ³ ἔσται γὰρ καιρὸς ὅτε τῆς ὑγιαινούσης διδασκαλίας οὐκ ἀνέξονται, ἀλλὰ κατὰ τὰς ἰδίας ἐπιθυμίας ἑαυτοῖς ἐπισωρεύσουσιν διδασκάλους κνηθόμενοι τὴν ἀκοήν, ⁴ καὶ ἀπὸ μὲν τῆς ἀληθείας τὴν ἀκοὴν ἀποστρέψουσιν, ἐπὶ δὲ τοὺς μύθους ἐκτραπήσονται. ⁵ σὺ δὲ νῆφε ἐν πᾶσιν, κακοπάθησον, ἔργον ποίησον εὐαγγελιστοῦ, τὴν διακονίαν σου πληροφόρησον. ⁶ Ἐγὼ γὰρ ἤδη σπένδομαι, καὶ ὁ καιρὸς τῆς ἀναλύσεώς μου ἐφέστηκεν. ⁷ τὸν καλὸν ἀγῶνα ἠγώνισμαι, τὸν δρόμον τετέλεκα, τὴν πίστιν τετήρηκα· ⁸ λοιπὸν ἀπόκειταί μοι ὁ τῆς δικαιοσύνης στέφανος, ὃν ἀποδώσει μοι ὁ κύριος ἐν ἐκείνῃ τῇ ἡμέρᾳ, ὁ δίκαιος κριτής, οὐ μόνον δὲ ἐμοὶ ἀλλὰ καὶ πᾶσιν τοῖς ἠγαπηκόσι τὴν ἐπιφάνειαν αὐτοῦ. ⁹ Σπούδασον ἐλθεῖν πρός με ταχέως· ¹⁰ Δημᾶς γάρ με ἐγκατέλιπεν ἀγαπήσας τὸν νῦν αἰῶνα, καὶ ἐπορεύθη εἰς Θεσσαλονίκην, Κρήσκης εἰς Γαλατίαν, Τίτος εἰς Δαλματίαν· ¹¹ Λουκᾶς ἐστιν μόνος μετ᾽ ἐμοῦ. Μᾶρκον ἀναλαβὼν ἄγε μετὰ σεαυτοῦ, ἔστιν γάρ μοι εὔχρηστος εἰς διακονίαν, ¹² Τυχικὸν δὲ ἀπέστειλα εἰς Ἔφεσον. ¹³ τὸν φαιλόνην, ὃν ἀπέλιπον ἐν Τρῳάδι παρὰ Κάρπῳ, ἐρχόμενος φέρε, καὶ τὰ βιβλία, μάλιστα τὰς μεμβράνας. ¹⁴ Ἀλέξανδρος ὁ χαλκεὺς πολλά μοι κακὰ ἐνεδείξατο— ἀποδώσει αὐτῷ ὁ κύριος κατὰ τὰ ἔργα αὐτοῦ— ¹⁵ ὃν καὶ σὺ φυλάσσου, λίαν γὰρ ἀντέστη τοῖς ἡμετέροις λόγοις. ¹⁶ Ἐν τῇ πρώτῃ μου ἀπολογίᾳ οὐδείς μοι παρεγένετο, ἀλλὰ πάντες με ἐγκατέλιπον— μὴ αὐτοῖς λογισθείη— ¹⁷ ὁ δὲ κύριός μοι παρέστη καὶ ἐνεδυνάμωσέν με, ἵνα δι᾽ ἐμοῦ τὸ κήρυγμα πληροφορηθῇ καὶ ἀκούσωσιν πάντα τὰ ἔθνη, καὶ ἐρρύσθην ἐκ στόματος λέοντος. ¹⁸ ῥύσεταί με ὁ κύριος ἀπὸ παντὸς ἔργου πονηροῦ καὶ σώσει εἰς τὴν βασιλείαν αὐτοῦ τὴν ἐπουράνιον· ᾧ ἡ δόξα εἰς τοὺς αἰῶνας τῶν αἰώνων, ἀμήν. ¹⁹ Ἄσπασαι Πρίσκαν καὶ Ἀκύλαν καὶ τὸν Ὀνησιφόρου οἶκον. ²⁰ Ἔραστος ἔμεινεν ἐν

Κορίνθῳ, Τρόφιμον δὲ ἀπέλιπον ἐν Μιλήτῳ ἀσθενοῦντα. ²¹ Σπούδασον πρὸ χειμῶνος ἐλθεῖν. Ἀσπάζεταί σε Εὔβουλος καὶ Πούδης καὶ Λίνος καὶ Κλαυδία καὶ οἱ ἀδελφοὶ πάντες.²² Ὁ κύριος μετὰ τοῦ πνεύματός σου. ἡ χάρις μεθ' ὑμῶν.

¹I charge you in the presence of God and of Christ Jesus who is to judge the living and the dead, and by his appearing and his kingdom: ²preach the word, be urgent in season and out of season, convince, rebuke, and exhort, be unfailing in patience and in teaching. ³For the time is coming when people will not endure sound teaching, but having itching ears they will accumulate for themselves teachers to suit their own likings, ⁴and will turn away from listening to the truth and wander into myths. ⁵As for you, always be steady, endure suffering, do the work of an evangelist, fulfil your ministry. ⁶For I am already on the point of being sacrificed; the time of my departure has come. ⁷I have fought the good fight, I have finished the race, I have kept the faith. ⁸Henceforth there is laid up for me the crown of righteousness, which the Lord, the righteous judge, will award to me on that Day, and not only to me but also to all who have loved his appearing. ⁹Do your best to come to me soon. ¹⁰For Demas, in love with this present world, has deserted me and gone to Thessalonica; Crescens has gone to Galatia, Titus to Dalmatia. ¹¹Luke alone is with me. Get Mark and bring him with you; for he is very useful in serving me. ¹²Tychicus I have sent to Ephesus. ¹³When you come, bring the cloak that I left with Carpus at Troas, also the books, and above all the parchments. ¹⁴Alexander the coppersmith did me great harm; the Lord will requite him for his deeds. ¹⁵Beware of him yourself, for he strongly opposed our message. ¹⁶At my first defense no one took my part; all deserted me. May it not be charged against them! ¹⁷But the Lord stood by me and gave me strength to proclaim the message fully, that all the Gentiles might hear it. So I was rescued from the lion's mouth. ¹⁸The Lord will rescue me from every evil and save me for his heavenly kingdom. To him be the glory for ever

2 Timothy: Chapter 4

and ever. Amen. ¹⁹*Greet Prisca and Aquila, and the household of Onesiphorus. ²⁰Erastus remained at Corinth; Trophimus I left ill at Miletus. ²¹Do your best to come before winter. Eubulus sends greetings to you, as do Pudens and Linus and Claudia and all the brethren. ²²The Lord be with your spirit. Grace be with you.*

Now that he is nearing the end of this letter conceived as a final testament,[1] Paul renews the charge he left with Timothy. This time, however, in view of the anticipated coming judgment, the appeal is phrased in a more encompassing manner that includes an exhaustive list of the duties for a bishop:

> In the presence of God and of Christ Jesus and of the elect angels I charge (*diamartyromai*; witness under oath) you to keep these rules without favor, doing nothing from partiality. (1 Tim 5:21)

> I charge (*diamartyromai*; witness under oath) you in the presence of God and of Christ Jesus who is to judge the living and the dead, and by his appearing and his kingdom: preach (*kēryxon*) the word, be urgent in season and out of season, convince, rebuke, and exhort, be unfailing in patience and in teaching. (2 Tim 4:1-2)

As previously pointed out, Paul added the title "teacher (*didaskalos*)" to "preacher (*kēryx*) and apostle" (1:11), titles reserved to an apostle like himself, to pressure the "teacher" Timothy to preserve the "(apostolic) teaching (*didaskalia*),"[2] and to remind him that he would have to carry on a task similar to that of Paul. The difference, however, is that Timothy would have to refer to the deposited writ rather than to speak the divine words as an apostle who heard those words *directly* from God himself:

> Paul an apostle—not from men nor through man, but through Jesus Christ and God the Father, who raised him from the dead—
> ... For I would have you know, brethren, that the gospel which was

---

[1] See earlier my comments on 2 Tim 1.
[2] For "teach" see 1 Tim 2:12; 6:2 (the infinitive present *didaskein*); 4:11 (the imperative *didaske*); 2 Tim 2:2 (the infinitive aorist *didaxai*); for "teaching" (*didaskalia*) see passim.

preached by me is not man's gospel. For I did not receive it from man, nor was I taught it, but it came through a revelation of Jesus Christ ... But when he who had set me apart before I was born, and had called me through his grace, was pleased to reveal his Son to me, in order that I might preach him among the Gentiles, I did not confer with flesh and blood, nor did I go up to Jerusalem to those who were apostles before me, but I went away into Arabia; and again I returned to Damascus. (Gal 1:1, 11-12, 15-17)

For I received from the Lord what I also delivered to you. (1 Cor 11:23a)[3]

In order to up the ante, instead of "lowering" himself to the status of "teacher," Paul "elevates" Timothy—without naming him apostle or preacher (*kēryx*)—by using the apostolic phrase *kēryssein ton logon* (preaching the word; 2 Tim 4:2) to refer to Timothy's teaching activity. The intention for doing this is sealed three verses later in the command: "*As for you*, always be steady, endure suffering (*kakopathēson*), do the work (*ergon*) of an evangelist (*evangelistou*), fulfil your ministry (*diakonian*; diaconate)." (v.5) Paul used *kakopathēson* twice earlier to invite Timothy to share in his suffering for the gospel's sake: "Do not be ashamed then of testifying to our Lord, nor of me his prisoner, but share in suffering (*synkakopathēson*) for the gospel in the power of God" (2 Tim 1:8); "Share in suffering (*Synkakopathēson*) as a good soldier of Christ Jesus." (2:3) Moreover, Paul refers to Timothy's mission as a ministry (*diakonia*), just as he often does when speaking of his own apostolic activity.

Nevertheless, Timothy's "work" is one of an "evangelist," not an apostle. The other two occurrences of "evangelist" in the New Testament are Acts 21:8, where Philip (the deacon [*diakonos*]; 6:5)

---

[3] One can also add the introductory formula to his letters "Paul, called by the will of God to be an apostle" (1 Cor 1:1; 2 Cor 1:1; Eph 1:1; Col 1:1; 1 Tim 1:1; 2 Tim 1:1).

is referred to as "evangelist" due to his missionary activity in chapter 8, and Ephesians:

> And his gifts were that some should be apostles, some prophets, some evangelists (*evangelistas*), some pastors (*poimenas*) and teachers (*didaskalous*), to equip the saints for the work (*ergon*) of ministry (*diakonias*), for building up the body of Christ. (4:11-12)

The similarity in phraseology between Ephesians and Timothy makes the connection in thought unmistakable, and thus one should use Ephesians to shed light on 2 Timothy, especially since the list in Ephesians expands on that found in 1 Corinthians:

> Now you are the body of Christ and individually members of it. And God has appointed (*etheto*) in the church first apostles, second prophets, third teachers, then workers of miracles, then healers, helpers, administrators, speakers in various kinds of tongues. (12:27-29)

It is evident that the inclusion of *evangelistas* is aimed at stretching the importance of that position to include all three facets of the episcopal function: the bishop is to *teach* his *flock* (as a "pastor" [shepherd] would) the *gospel* message. The view of the bishop as pastor is corroborated in Paul's address to the leaders of the church of Ephesus, where Timothy is bishop:

> And from Miletus he sent to Ephesus and called to him the elders (*presbyterous*) of the church. And when they came to him, he said to them: "You yourselves know how I lived among you all the time from the first day that I set foot in Asia ... Take heed (*prosekhete*)[4] to yourselves and to all the flock (*poimniō*), in which the Holy Spirit has made (*etheto*;[5] appointed) you overseers (*episkopous*), to care for the church of God which he obtained with the blood of his own Son. I know that after my departure fierce wolves will come in

---

[4] Compare with 1 Tim 4:13: "Till I come, attend to (*prosekhe*) the public reading of scripture, to preaching, to teaching."
[5] The same verb as in 1 Cor 11:28.

among you, not sparing the flock (*poimniou*); and from among your own selves will arise men speaking perverse things, to draw away the disciples after them." (Acts 20:17-18, 28-30).

Now that Paul has accomplished the mission for which he was called, "to proclaim the message fully (*to kerygma plērophorēthē*), that *all the Gentiles* might hear it" (2 Tim 4:17), both aloud as "heralding" (*kerygma*; preaching by mouth) and as a "deposit" (*parathēkē*) in his letters, he considers that "I have fought the good fight, I have finished the race" (v.7) and, consequently, that "the time of my departure has come" (v.6) and "henceforth there is laid up for me the crown of righteousness, which the Lord, the righteous judge, will award to me on that Day, and not only to me but also to all who have loved his appearing" (v.8). All that remains is for him to give his final directives to Timothy, his heir apparent. What is striking in this regard is his first statement, "Do your best (*Spoudason*) to come to me soon (*takheōs*)" (v.9). A keen ear will realize that the earlier and only other use of *spoudason* is found in the same context of judgment: "Do your best (*spoudason*) to present yourself (*parastēsai*; stand before [as in court of law])[6] to God as one approved (*dokimon*; passing muster [when judged]),[7] a workman who has no need to be ashamed, rightly handling the word of truth." (2:15) Paul prepared for 4:9 by including, along with himself, "all who have loved his [the Lord's] appearing" in v.8. In v.9 he is preparing Timothy for the same fate as his, since Timothy's task is to hand down to his followers the "deposit" inscribed in 1 and 2 Timothy as well as in the other Pauline letters. This, in turn, explains why Paul glosses over Timothy and moves on to the long and, as we shall see, all-inclusive list of Timothy's companions who will have to both abide by and teach this "deposit."

---

[6] See my comments on this verb in *C-Rom* 226; *C-2Cor* 195.
[7] See my comments on this adjective in *C-Rom* 107; *C-1Cor* 202-3; *C-2Cor* 162-3, 180, 190, 225-6.

This list is obviously meant to be programmatic in the same way as the extended list of Romans 16.[8] It works on two levels at the same time. The first is to establish the New Testament canon as an integral part of the "deposit."[9] Secondly, following the lead of Romans 9-11, it is meant to subdue the potential arrogance of the Gentiles against the Jews opposing Paul and his gospel by assuming that they, the Gentiles, are better off. The matter is pushed to the extreme in that what was offered as a possibility in Romans 11 is presented here as factuality: Gentiles are betraying Paul. Even more, whereas in Romans the Jews are cast in terms of the scriptural Israel that were disobedient to the deposited message of the Old Testament canon, here it is the named Gentiles who are turning their backs on the deposited message of the New Testament canon. In other words, Gentiles have proven to be worse off than Jews! This point is actually put in relief when the hearer compares the earlier "But if *some* of the branches [representing Jews] were broken off, and you [representing Gentiles], a wild olive shoot, were grafted in their place to share the richness of the olive tree" (Rom 11:17) with the last statement concerning the Gentiles in 2 Timothy 4:16: "At my first defense *no one* took my part; *all* deserted me."

The inclusiveness of the desertion is evident. The entire passage covering the first list of names (2 Tim 4:9-16) is bracketed by a reference to "leaving someone on his own," accounting for the only instances of the verb *enkataleipein* in the Pastoral Epistles, "Demas ... has deserted (*enkatelipen*) me" (v.10) and "all deserted (*enkatelipon*) me" (v.16). In the original, verse 10 presages verse 16 in that the name *Dēmas* is from the Greek *dēmos* meaning people, (common) crowd, and thus reflective of the totality. However, the action of Demas contrasts with that of Luke who remained with Paul (v.11), and thus breaks the intimate harmony

---

[8] See my detailed discussion in *C-Rom* 270-87.
[9] This is the case in Colossians 4:7-18; see my comments in *C-Col* 94-106.

between the two described earlier in Colossians: "Luke the beloved physician (*iatros*) and Demas greet you." (4:14) The Greek *Loukas* (Luke) is the rendering of the Latin *Lucius* or *Lucianus*, a person that enlightens others. Taken in combination with *Dēmas*, the two names symbolize the message of the gospel that carries the light of the Law and its teaching to the Gentiles (Rom 2:17-20). This reading is supported by the fact that Luke is qualified by *iatros*, meaning the one who heals those in need of that healing. In the Gospels, Christ's teaching is often cast as a healing.[10] More apropos, in Luke, Christ the teacher refers to himself in a parabolic statement as a "physician" (*iatre*; 4:23). Moreover, in the Gospels, the highest incidence of the verb *iaomai* (heal), from the same root as *iatros*, is found in Luke.[11] The noun *iasis* (healing) from the same root, occurs only in Luke-Acts (Lk 13:32; Acts 4:22, 30[12]). The centrality of this symbolism is corroborated in that, among the Evangelists, only Luke speaks of God's household as a *therapeia* (house of healing, healing institution; 12:42[13]), and explicates Jesus' teaching about the kingdom of God as being a *therapeia* (healing) unto those who need it (9:11).[14] The betrayal of the gospel among Gentiles is underscored by the inclusion of two other names between Demas and Luke: Crescens and Titus. The first, *Krēskēs*, is the Greek rendition of the Latin *Crescens* whose meaning is "growing, multiplying," while Titus is a clear reference to the emperor of that name and, by extension, to Roman imperial power. So the combination of the names Demas, Crescens, and Titus, in that order, reflects Gentiles becoming

---

[10] Mt 4:23; 9:35; 10:1, 7-8; 13:14-15; Mk 6:2-5, 6a-13; Lk 4:14-30; 6:6-10; 9:1-2, 6, 11; 10:9; 13:10-12.

[11] Eleven times in Lk (+ 4 times in Acts) compared to thrice in Mt (+ once in a quotation from Is 6:10 in Mt 13:15), once in Mk, and twice in Jn (+ once in the same Isaianic quotation in Jn 12:40).

[12] The original *eis iasin* (unto healing) is translated as "to heal" (RSV).

[13] RSV erroneously translates the original *therapeias* as "household" to make it corresponding the Matthean parallel that has *oiketias* (household; Mat 24:45).

[14] The latter understanding is found also in Rev 22:2 where the leaves of the tree of life in the heavenly Jerusalem are said to be "for the healing (*eis therapeian*) of the nations."

enamored with Roman power over and against the gospel teaching which is represented by Luke. Taken together, they smack of the connotation of the pair Hymemaeus and Alexander (1 Tim 1:20).[15] That the author had the latter in mind is evident in the unexpected mention of Alexander the coppersmith a few verses later (2 Tim 4:14).

Immediately after Luke we hear of Mark, whose name is linked with the earliest Gospel. In Colossians 4:7-18 these two names appear together in a context where the New Testament canon is introduced.[16] However, in that epistle, while Luke was introduced succinctly as well as positively (Luke the beloved physician; v.14), Mark had to be rehabilitated because he turned his back on the mission to the Gentiles at first (Acts 15:37-40): "Mark the cousin of Barnabas (concerning whom you have received instructions—if he comes to you, receive him)." (v.10)[17] Here also we hear the same tone since Paul had to give Timothy a reason to "bring Mark *with you*": "for he is very useful (*evkhrēstos*) in serving me (*eis diakonian*; unto [the] ministry [of table fellowship]" (v.11), which is the Pauline gospel.[18]

Luke and Mark function as the Evangelists, and thus they represent their respective Gospels. This is confirmed in the following verses where, together with Mark, Timothy is summoned in the following terms: "When you come (soon; v. 9), bring (together with Mark; v.11) the cloak (*phailonēn*) that I left with Carpus (*Karpō*; dative of *Karpos*) at Troas, also the books (*biblia*), and above all the parchments (*membranas*)." (v.13) This verse is arguably the most pregnant statement in scripture since it works simultaneously on different levels. By summoning Timothy to "come to me soon" (v.9), Paul is indicating that Timothy's

---

[15] See earlier my comments on that verse.
[16] See my comments in *C-Col* 94-106.
[17] See my comments in *C-Col* 94-106.
[18] See my comments on Onesiphorus/Onesimus in chapter 1. See also *C-2Cor* 73-86.

mission in Ephesus is accomplished. This is made clear in the otherwise unexpected v.10: "Tychicus I have sent (*apesteila*)[19] to Ephesus." The Greek *Tykhikos* means "fortuitous, chosen by fate" and thus indicates anyone who would be assigned at God's discretion; the corollary is that Timothy should not worry about the future, which is in (God's) "good hands."[20] In fact, Timothy is not to worry at all since the Pauline gospel to Gentiles that originated in Troas[21] has borne fruit, which is the meaning of the Greek *karpos* (v.13). If Paul's apostolic mission has both ended and borne fruit, all that remains is that his school—Timothy, Luke, and Mark—gather together around him, that is, around the one who wears "*the* cloak" (*ton phailonēn*)[22] of the master, and more importantly to gather around *the written* apostolic legacy— "*the* parchments" (*tas membranas*)[23]—that are comparable to those of the Old Testament and are already preserved as "*the* books" (*ta biblia*). Precedence given to the written material over the teacher has been prepared for in the earlier mention of Moses (3:8) who died (Josh 1:1)—just as Paul's fate is about to be—before the entrance into the earth of promise, which took place under the banner of the Book of the Law (Josh 3-4). What is further striking is the differentiation between "the books" and "the parchments." The latter does not necessarily mean individual pages since "the books" (*ta biblia*) is a technical reference to the Old Testament scriptures as is clear from the following instances:

> Therefore, though we have no need of these things, since we have as encouragement the holy books which are in our hands, (2 Macc 12:9)

---

[19] Form the verb *apostellō* whence *apostolos* (apostle).
[20] See further my comments in *C-Col* 95-6.
[21] See my detailed comments in *C-2Cor* 39-45 and 64-5 on the function of that city in scripture.
[22] Unique instance in the entire scripture.
[23] Unique instance in the entire scripture.

Whereas many great teachings have been given to us through the law and the prophets and the others that followed them, on account of which we should praise Israel for instruction and wisdom; and since it is necessary not only that the readers themselves should acquire understanding but also that those who love learning should be able to help the outsiders by both speaking and writing, my grandfather Jesus, after devoting himself especially to the reading of the law and the prophets and the other books of our fathers, and after acquiring considerable proficiency in them, was himself also led to write something pertaining to instruction and wisdom, in order that, by becoming conversant with this also, those who love learning should make even greater progress in living according to the law.

You are urged therefore to read with good will and attention, and to be indulgent in cases where, despite our diligent labor in translating, we may seem to have rendered some phrases imperfectly. For what was originally expressed in Hebrew does not have exactly the same sense when translated into another language. Not only this work, but even the law itself, the prophecies, and the rest of the books differ not a little as originally expressed.

When I came to Egypt in the thirty-eighth year of the reign of Euergetes and stayed for some time, I found opportunity for no little instruction. It seemed highly necessary that I should myself devote some pains and labor to the translation of the following book, using in that period of time great watchfulness and skill in order to complete and publish the book for those living abroad who wished to gain learning, being prepared in character to live according to the law. (Preamble to Ecclesiasticus)

The differentiation between "the parchments" and "the books" parallels that of Paul's epistles and the scriptures, mention of which is found at the end of 2 Peter:

Therefore, beloved, since you wait for these, be zealous to be found by him without spot or blemish, and at peace. And count the forbearance of our Lord as salvation. So also our beloved brother

Paul wrote to you according to the wisdom given him, speaking of this as he does in all his letters. There are some things in them hard to understand, which the ignorant and unstable twist to their own destruction, as they do the other scriptures. (2 Pet 3:14-16)

Paul's assuredness of the success of the gospel (2 Tim 4:16-18) is always on hope; that is why it does not preclude further attacks by Gentiles whom Paul has evangelized, including the like of Alexander (vv.14-15). In order to impress upon Timothy his hope in the fullness of his mission among the Gentiles, Paul brings into the picture his rescue from the lion's mouth, an example that applies to his personal experience in no less than Ephesus itself, i.e., Timothy's episcopal sea: "What do I gain if, humanly speaking, I fought with beasts at Ephesus?" (1 Cor 15:32a); "For we do not want you to be ignorant, brethren, of the affliction we experienced in Asia; for we were so utterly, unbearably crushed that we despaired of life itself." (2 Cor 1:8)[24] More importantly, the scriptural example of being rescued from the lion's mouth is found in conjunction with someone who suffered such while administering the wisdom of the Law to Gentile kings. Daniel 6:16-24 has become the classic example of this metaphor, as witnessed by its reiteration in 1 Maccabees: "Daniel because of his innocence was delivered from the mouth of the lions." (2:60)[25] Both the scriptural precedent and Paul's own experience in having been rescued repeatedly by God[26] allows him to be confident that God will continue to do this in the future until the end of days: "The Lord will rescue (*rhysetai*) me from every evil and save me

---

[24] These two examples brings to mind a fight against wild animals in the Roman arena.
[25] Actually it is this verse that seems to be on Paul's mind since they both use the same verb *errysthē(n)* from *rhyomai*, whereas it is the verb *exaireō* that is found repeatedly in the passage from Daniel.
[26] "Now you have observed my teaching, my conduct, my aim in life, my faith, my patience, my love, my steadfastness, my persecutions, my sufferings, what befell me at Antioch, at Iconium, and at Lystra, what persecutions I endured; yet from them all the Lord rescued (*errysato*) me." (2 Tim 3:10-11)

for his heavenly kingdom. To him be the glory for ever and ever. Amen." (2 Tim 4:18)[27]

Thus, in order to stress the point that his farewell (2 Tim 4:6-8) is indeed final, Paul invites Timothy to realize that his time is practically over. The "deposit" has been established, and all that Timothy has to do is point his followers to it. In any case, Timothy is no greater than Moses or Paul; if those two are bound to fade away behind their permanent writings, how much more is Timothy, who did not leave a written legacy, bound to fade away. Yet the light of the Pauline *written* gospel will remain forever in spite of the desertions from it (v.8) and the attacks against it (vv.14-18).

As I indicated many times in my commentaries, in a literature meant to be heard, the author underscores an important point by repeating it.[28] That is why Paul twice formulates his request for Timothy to join him (vv.9 and 21) and each time he does so in conjunction with a cluster of names (vv.10-18 and 19-22). However, compared with the first list of names, the second list, which is divided in two by the request for Timothy to "come," is totally positive in tone. Still, the two parts seem to function differently given that the four names of the first list are otherwise known in the New Testament, whereas the four names of the second list occur only here.

If Prisca and Aquila together with Onesiphorus and his household are to be greeted by Timothy (v.19), this means they are in Ephesus; and if so, then Timothy truly need not worry about the future of his church since it is in the best possible of hands. Therefore he could "come" to join Paul with total peace of mind. Prisca is an adjective meaning "pristine, age old, original"

---

[27] The intentional link between 2 Tim 3:10-11, 4:17, and 4:18 is evident in that these account for all instances of the verb *rhyomai* in this epistle.
[28] School teachers use this device often in their classes.

and Aquila is "eagle." Between them, they represented the Roman empire as well as old Rome from its beginning to the rise of the empire. Prisca and Aquila were so well tamed by the Pauline gospel in Corinth (Acts 18:1-4) that he took them with him to Ephesus (vv.18-19) where they proved their value as well as commitment "by expounding the way of God more accurately" to no less than Apollos (v.26) to the extent that he became Paul's co-minister in Corinth (1 Cor 3). Onesiphorus, discussed earlier (2 Tim 1:16), was shown to be none other than the highly praised Onesimus (Philem 8-19). The fact that both times he is referred to with his household means that he has become a major leader in the house church of Philemon (v.2) whose importance is evident in that Paul dedicated a letter to him. Furthermore, Paul impresses upon Timothy that he did not forget Corinth, the capital of the Roman province Achaia, since he left there none other than Erastus, whose Greek name *Erastos* (from the root *eros* [love]) means "amiable, one who loves," and thus personifies the Pauline gospel. Erastus equals in value Timothy himself: "Now after these events Paul resolved in the Spirit to pass through Macedonia and Achaia and go to Jerusalem, saying, 'After I have been there, I must also see Rome.' And having sent into Macedonia two of his helpers (*diakonountōn*),[29] Timothy and Erastus, he himself stayed in Asia for a while." (Acts 19:21-22). Titus, who accompanied Paul to Jerusalem (Gal 2:1, 3) as a showcase and ended up deserting him (2 Tim 4:10), is now replaced with Trophimus, who also accompanied Paul to Jerusalem (Acts 21:29). He is a close companion of both Timothy and Tychicus (20:4) and of Paul

---

[29]This denomination puts Erastus on par with all three, Paul (I thank him who has given me strength for this, Christ Jesus our Lord, because he judged me faithful by appointing me to his service [*diakonian*]; 1 Tim 1:12), Timothy (As for you, always be steady, endure suffering, do the work of an evangelist, fulfil your ministry [*diakonian*]; 2 Tim 4:5), and Mark (Get Mark and bring him with you; for he is very useful in serving [*diakonian*] me; v.11).

himself (21:29). Trophimus is assigned to Miletus, which is where Paul summoned the elders of Ephesus for his farewell speech (20:17-18). Although he is ill (2 Tim 4:20b), Trophimus, as his Greek name *Trophimos* connotes, is still able to "feed" those around him with the gospel word, just as his master was able to do in Galatia and in Corinth:

> You know it was because of a bodily ailment that I preached the gospel to you at first; and though my condition was a trial to you, you did not scorn or despise me, but received me as an angel of God, as Christ Jesus. (Gal 4:13-14)

> We are treated as impostors, and yet are true; as unknown, and yet well known; as dying, and behold we live; as punished, and yet not killed; as sorrowful, yet always rejoicing; as poor, yet making many rich; as having nothing, and yet possessing everything. (2 Cor 6:8b-10)

At this point, one would expect Paul to end the letter with his traditional closing, "The Lord be with your spirit. Grace be with you" (2 Tim 4:22), so the preceding verse, "Do your best to come before winter. Eubulus sends greetings to you, as do Pudens and Linus and Claudia and all the brethren" seems peculiar. It is odd on two levels. On the one hand, all four names are unique in the New Testament and, as such, do not seem to add much to the preceding. On the other hand, why would Paul repeat his request to Timothy, which he had done earlier (v.9), with the seemingly ominous addition of "before winter"? In order to unravel the apparent conundrum of this self-standing verse, I propose that both sentences be taken together in such a way that one would explain the other. The only instances of winter being threatening are in Mark 13:18 and its parallel Matthew 24:20,[30] where it is

---

[30] The priority of Mark over Matthew is well established. In our case, it is evident in that Matthew adds "or on a sabbath" after Mark's original "in winter": "then let those who are in Judea flee to the mountains … Pray that it may not happen in winter" (Mk 13:14,

connected with the coming of the Lord and the final judgment. In both cases the coming of the Lord is contingent on the gospel having been preached to all nations: "And the gospel must first be preached to all nations" (Mk 13:10); "And this gospel of the kingdom will be preached throughout the whole world, as a testimony to all nations; and then the end will come." (Mt 24:14). This scenario fits perfectly the verse we are discussing. The four names—an alternating combination of two Greek names, Eubulus and Linus, and two Latin (Roman) names, Pudens and Claudia—are clearly representative of all nations, given that the numeral four connotes universalism. It is because his gospel message has reached all nations that Paul is prodding Timothy to hurry up and join him before winter. This argument acquires more pertinence when one remembers that Timothy has been asked to bring the parchments Paul had left at Troas and to bring Mark, the author of one of them.[31]

---

18); "then let those who are in Judea flee to the mountains ... Pray that your flight may not be in winter or on a sabbath." (Mt 24:16, 20)

[31] See my comments on 2 Tim 4:9, 11, 13.

Titus

Chapter 1

Vv. 1-16 ¹Παῦλος δοῦλος θεοῦ, ἀπόστολος δὲ Ἰησοῦ Χριστοῦ κατὰ πίστιν ἐκλεκτῶν θεοῦ καὶ ἐπίγνωσιν ἀληθείας τῆς κατ᾽ εὐσέβειαν ² ἐπ᾽ ἐλπίδι ζωῆς αἰωνίου, ἣν ἐπηγγείλατο ὁ ἀψευδὴς θεὸς πρὸ χρόνων αἰωνίων ³ ἐφανέρωσεν δὲ καιροῖς ἰδίοις, τὸν λόγον αὐτοῦ ἐν κηρύγματι ὃ ἐπιστεύθην ἐγὼ κατ᾽ ἐπιταγὴν τοῦ σωτῆρος ἡμῶν θεοῦ, ⁴ Τίτῳ γνησίῳ τέκνῳ κατὰ κοινὴν πίστιν· χάρις καὶ εἰρήνη ἀπὸ θεοῦ πατρὸς καὶ Χριστοῦ Ἰησοῦ τοῦ σωτῆρος ἡμῶν.⁵ Τούτου χάριν ἀπέλιπόν σε ἐν Κρήτῃ ἵνα τὰ λείποντα ἐπιδιορθώσῃ, καὶ καταστήσῃς κατὰ πόλιν πρεσβυτέρους, ὡς ἐγώ σοι διεταξάμην, ⁶ εἴ τίς ἐστιν ἀνέγκλητος, μιᾶς γυναικὸς ἀνήρ, τέκνα ἔχων πιστά, μὴ ἐν κατηγορίᾳ ἀσωτίας ἢ ἀνυπότακτα. ⁷ δεῖ γὰρ τὸν ἐπίσκοπον ἀνέγκλητον εἶναι ὡς θεοῦ οἰκονόμον, μὴ αὐθάδη, μὴ ὀργίλον, μὴ πάροινον, μὴ πλήκτην, μὴ αἰσχροκερδῆ, ⁸ ἀλλὰ φιλόξενον, φιλάγαθον, σώφρονα, δίκαιον, ὅσιον, ἐγκρατῆ, ⁹ ἀντεχόμενον τοῦ κατὰ τὴν διδαχὴν πιστοῦ λόγου, ἵνα δυνατὸς ᾖ καὶ παρακαλεῖν ἐν τῇ διδασκαλίᾳ τῇ ὑγιαινούσῃ καὶ τοὺς ἀντιλέγοντας ἐλέγχειν.¹⁰ Εἰσὶν γὰρ πολλοὶ καὶ ἀνυπότακτοι, ματαιολόγοι καὶ φρεναπάται, μάλιστα οἱ ἐκ τῆς περιτομῆς, ¹¹ οὓς δεῖ ἐπιστομίζειν, οἵτινες ὅλους οἴκους ἀνατρέπουσιν διδάσκοντες ἃ μὴ δεῖ αἰσχροῦ κέρδους χάριν. ¹² εἶπέν τις ἐξ αὐτῶν, ἴδιος αὐτῶν προφήτης, Κρῆτες ἀεὶ ψεῦσται, κακὰ θηρία, γαστέρες ἀργαί· ¹³ ἡ μαρτυρία αὕτη ἐστὶν ἀληθής. δι᾽ ἣν αἰτίαν ἔλεγχε αὐτοὺς ἀποτόμως, ἵνα ὑγιαίνωσιν ἐν τῇ πίστει, ¹⁴ μὴ προσέχοντες Ἰουδαϊκοῖς μύθοις καὶ ἐντολαῖς ἀνθρώπων ἀποστρεφομένων τὴν ἀλήθειαν. ¹⁵ πάντα καθαρὰ τοῖς καθαροῖς· τοῖς δὲ μεμιαμμένοις καὶ ἀπίστοις οὐδὲν καθαρόν, ἀλλὰ μεμίανται αὐτῶν καὶ ὁ νοῦς καὶ ἡ συνείδησις. ¹⁶ θεὸν ὁμολογοῦσιν εἰδέναι, τοῖς δὲ ἔργοις ἀρνοῦνται, βδελυκτοὶ ὄντες καὶ ἀπειθεῖς καὶ πρὸς πᾶν ἔργον ἀγαθὸν ἀδόκιμοι.

¹*Paul, a servant of God and an apostle of Jesus Christ, to further the faith of God's elect and their knowledge of the truth which accords with godliness,* ²*in hope of eternal life which God, who*

never lies, promised ages ago ³and at the proper time manifested in his word through the preaching with which I have been entrusted by command of God our Savior; ⁴To Titus, my true child in a common faith: Grace and peace from God the Father and Christ Jesus our Savior. ⁵This is why I left you in Crete, that you might amend what was defective, and appoint elders in every town as I directed you, ⁶if any man is blameless, the husband of one wife, and his children are believers and not open to the charge of being profligate or insubordinate. ⁷For a bishop, as God's steward, must be blameless; he must not be arrogant or quick-tempered or a drunkard or violent or greedy for gain, ⁸but hospitable, a lover of goodness, master of himself, upright, holy, and self-controlled; ⁹he must hold firm to the sure word as taught, so that he may be able to give instruction in sound doctrine and also to confute those who contradict it. ¹⁰For there are many insubordinate men, empty talkers and deceivers, especially the circumcision party; ¹¹they must be silenced, since they are upsetting whole families by teaching for base gain what they have no right to teach. ¹²One of themselves, a prophet of their own, said, "Cretans are always liars, evil beasts, lazy gluttons." ¹³This testimony is true. Therefore rebuke them sharply, that they may be sound in the faith, ¹⁴instead of giving heed to Jewish myths or to commands of men who reject the truth. ¹⁵To the pure all things are pure, but to the corrupt and unbelieving nothing is pure; their very minds and consciences are corrupted. ¹⁶They profess to know God, but they deny him by their deeds; they are detestable, disobedient, unfit for any good deed.

The first question that comes to mind in conjunction with this epistle is, "Why would Paul reward Titus who "deserted him" (2 Tim 4:10) with the same honor and divine commission as Timothy?" The answer to this will only become clear when the function of this letter is unlocked through an exegesis of the epistle itself. Since this epistle sounds like a repeat of the main points of the preceding two letters, it is only by zeroing in on its peculiarities that we can hope to find out why it was written.[1]

In the two previous letters not only does Paul introduce himself as "apostle" (1 Tim 1:1; 2 Tim 1:1), but he repeats this in the body of the letter (1 Tim 2:7; 2 Tim 1:11). He does the same in the greeting to Titus, however, he preambles this by referring to himself as "servant (*doulos*; slave) of God" (Tit 1:1). This is a unique depiction in the New Testament, whether of Paul or of anyone else. To be sure, Paul speaks of himself several times as "servant (*doulos*; slave) of Jesus Christ" (Rom 1:1; Phil 1:1; see also Gal 1:10), but never as a "servant (*doulos*; slave) of God." What makes this striking is that the more common "apostle of Jesus Christ" that immediately follows this appellation is relegated to a secondary status.[2] We find "servant of God" only two other times in the New Testament, once to qualify James (Jas 1:1) and the other in reference to Moses (Rev 15:3). Since James is the leader of the Jewish Christian community and Moses is the giver of the Law, it is only fitting that they would be introduced as the servants of God, the Old Testament deity. It is also fitting of Paul inasmuch as he was "called to be an apostle, set apart for the gospel of God which he promised beforehand through his prophets *in the holy scriptures*" (Rom 1:1-2). This parallel thought in Romans concerning Paul's message as well as his mission links that epistle with Titus:

> Paul, a *servant* of God and an *apostle of Jesus Christ*, to further the *faith* of God's elect and their knowledge of the truth which accords with godliness, in hope of eternal life which *God*, who never lies, *promised* (*epēngeilato*) *ages ago* (*pro khronōn aiōniōn*; before times

---

[1] Moreover, it would be tedious to go over the similarities, especially after having covered them twice in the letters to Timothy.
[2] The original *doulos Theou, apostolos de Iēsou Khristou* is literally rendered as "servant of God, yet (and also; however also; and on the other hand) apostle of Jesus Christ."

immemorial) and at the proper time manifested in his word *through the preaching with which I have been entrusted* by command of God our Savior. (Tit 1:1-3)

Paul, a *servant* of Jesus Christ, called to be an *apostle*, set apart for the gospel of *God* which he *promised beforehand* (*proepēngeilato*)³ through his prophets in the holy scriptures, the gospel concerning … *Jesus Christ* our Lord, *through whom we have received* grace and *apostleship* to bring about the obedience of *faith* for the sake of his name among all the nations, including yourselves who are called to belong to Jesus Christ. (Rom 1:1-6)

Keeping in mind that the gospel expounded in Romans "is the power of God for salvation to every one who has faith, to the Jew first and also to the Greek" (1:16) will help us understand another idiosyncrasy. The phrase "common (*koinēn*) faith" (Tit 1:5) occurs only here in the entire New Testament. The usual meaning of the comparatively rarely used adjective *koinēn*, and the equally rare cognate verb *koinoō*, is "common, regular, not special," in the scriptural sense of being "impure, unclean, defiled" versus the "pure, clean, set apart, select, special":

Now when the Pharisees gathered together to him, with some of the scribes, who had come from Jerusalem, they saw that some of his disciples ate with hands defiled (*koinais*), that is, unwashed. (For the Pharisees, and all the Jews, do not eat unless they wash their hands, observing the tradition of the elders; and when they come from the

---

³ Notice how this verb integrates the Greek preposition *pro* (before) that follows the verb "promised" (*epēngeilato*) in Titus. This is the only instance of the verbal conjugation *proepēngeilato* in the New Testament. The verb itself is found only once more as adjectival participle *proepēngelmenēn* in 2 Cor 9:5 where the agent of the promise is not God: "So I thought it necessary to urge the brethren to go on to you before me, and arrange in advance for this gift *you have promised* (your gift promised beforehand), so that it may be ready not as an exaction but as a willing gift."

market place, they do not eat unless they purify themselves; and there are many other traditions which they observe, the washing of cups and pots and vessels of bronze.) And the Pharisees and the scribes asked him, "Why do your disciples not live according to the tradition of the elders, but eat with hands defiled (*koinais*)?" And he said to them ... "You leave the commandment (*entolēn*) of God, and hold fast *the tradition of men*." And he said to them, "You have a fine way of rejecting the commandment (*entolēn*) of God, in order to keep your tradition! For Moses said, 'Honor your father and your mother'; and, 'He who speaks evil of father or mother, let him surely die'; but you say, 'If a man tells his father or his mother, What you would have gained from me is Corban' (that is, given to God)— then you no longer permit him to do anything for his father or mother, thus *making void (akyrountes)*[4] *the word of God* through your tradition which you hand on. And many such things you do." And he called the people to him again, and said to them, "Hear me, all of you, and understand: there is nothing outside a man which by going into him can defile (*koinōsai*) him; but the things which come out of a man are what defile (*koinounta*) him."[5] And when he had entered the house, and left the people, his disciples asked him about the parable. And he said to them, "Then are you also without understanding? Do you not see that whatever goes into a man from outside cannot defile (*koinōsai*) him, since it enters, not his heart but his stomach, and so passes on?" (Thus he *declared* all foods *clean* [*katharizōn*][6].) And he said, "What comes out of a man is what defiles (*koinoi*) a man. For from within, out of the heart of man, come evil thoughts, fornication, theft, murder, adultery, coveting, wickedness, deceit, licentiousness, envy, slander, pride, foolishness.

---

[4] Besides the Matthean parallel (Mt 15:6), the verb *akyroō* occurs once more, exclusively in Galatians: "This is what I mean: the law, which came four hundred and thirty years afterward, does not annul a covenant previously ratified by God, so as to make the promise void." (3:17)

[5] Compare with Tit 1:14: "To the pure (*kathara*) all things are pure (*katharois*), but to the corrupt and unbelieving nothing is pure (*katharon*); their very minds and consciences are corrupted."

[6] This is from the same root as *kathara*, *katharois*, and *katharon* of the quotation in the previous footnote.

All these evil things come from within, and they defile (*koinoi*) a man." (Mk 7:1-6, 8-15, 17-23)

"not what goes into the mouth defiles (*koinoi*) a man, but what comes out of the mouth, this defiles (*koinoi*) a man" ... "Do you not see that whatever goes into the mouth passes into the stomach, and so passes on? But what comes out of the mouth proceeds from the heart, and this defiles (*koinoi*) a man. For out of the heart come evil thoughts, murder, adultery, fornication, theft, false witness, slander. These are what defile (*ta koinounta*) a man; but to eat with unwashed hands does not defile (*koinoi*) a man." (Mt 15:11, 17-20)

I know and am persuaded in the Lord Jesus that nothing is unclean (*koinon*) in itself; but it is unclean for any one who thinks it unclean (*koinon*). (Rom 14:14)

But nothing unclean (*koinon*) shall enter it [the city that descended from heaven], nor any one who practices abomination or falsehood, but only those who are written in the Lamb's book of life. (Rev 21:27)

The noun *koinōnia*, connoting "table fellowship, common table" as well as "fellowship in general, holding things in common," especially between Jews and Gentiles, is at the heart of the Pauline gospel teaching starting with Galatians 2:11-14. Luke capitalized on this in his Book of Acts:

And all who believed were together and had all things *in common* (*epi to avto*) and they sold their possessions and goods and distributed them to all, as any had need. (Acts 2:44-45)

Now the company of those who believed were of one heart and soul, and no one said that any of the things which he possessed was his own, but they had everything in common (*koina*). (4:32)

And he became hungry and desired something to eat; but while they were preparing it, he fell into a trance and saw the heaven opened, and something descending, like a great sheet, let down by four corners upon the earth. In it were all kinds of animals and reptiles and birds of the air. And there came a voice to him, "Rise, Peter; kill and eat." But Peter said, "No, Lord; for I have never eaten anything that is common (*koinon*) or unclean (*akatharton*)." And the voice came to him again a second time, "What God has cleansed, you must not *call common* (*koinou* [imperative of the verb *koinoō*])." This happened three times, and the thing was taken up at once to heaven. (10:10-16)

and he said to them, "You yourselves know how unlawful it is for a Jew to associate with or to visit any one of another nation; but God has shown me that I should not call any man common (*koinon*) or unclean (*akatharton*)." (10:28)

And I heard a voice saying to me, "Rise, Peter; kill and eat." But I said, "No, Lord; for nothing common (*koinon*) or unclean (*akatharton*) has ever entered my mouth." But the voice answered a second time from heaven, "What God has cleansed you must not *call common* (*koinou*)." This happened three times, and all was drawn up again into heaven. (11:7-10)

However, the "common faith" (Tit 1:4), which is assumed beyond 1 and 2 Timothy, is the Pauline gospel that Titus himself witnessed in action at the Jerusalem meeting (Gal 2:1-10). This is confirmed a few verses later (Tit 1:10) where reference is made to "the circumcision party" (*hoi ek tēs peritomēs*). The noun "circumcision" is not found in the previous Pastoral Letters, and the phrase "the circumcision party" occurs exclusively in conjunction with the aftermath of the Jerusalem meeting in Antioch (Gal 2:12) and with Peter's defense of the Pauline understanding of the inclusiveness of the gospel (Acts 10:45; 11:2), which is a corrective to his betrayal at Antioch (Gal 2:11-14). The Galatians connection is corroborated in that "the circumcision party" in Titus are accused of "giving heed to Jewish (*Ioudaikois*) myths or to commands (*entolais*; commandments) of men" (1:14) and of differentiating between "pure" (*kathara*) and "impure" (v.15). The unique instance of the adjective *Ioudaikois* is found elsewhere in its adverbial form *Ioudaikōs* (in a Jewish manner; like a Jew) only in Gal 2:14: "But when I saw that they were not straightforward about the truth of the gospel, I said to Cephas before them all, 'If you, though a Jew, live like a Gentile and not *like a Jew* (*Ioudaikōs*), how can you compel the Gentiles to live like Jews?'" The "commands of men" and "pure" recall the episode where Jesus criticized the "tradition of the elders" in Mark (7:1-23), a story based on the episode at Antioch in Galatians (2:11-14)[7] referred to earlier in the discussion of the adjective *koinon*.

In the letters to Timothy the phrase *pistos ho logos* (the [gospel] word is sure; the saying is faithful) is usually followed with a description of the content of that "word":

> The saying is sure and worthy of full acceptance, that Christ Jesus came into the world to *save* (*sōsai*) sinners. And I am the foremost of sinners; but I received mercy for this reason, that in me, as the foremost, Jesus Christ might display his perfect patience for an example to *those who were to believe* (*pistevein*) in him for eternal life. (1 Tim 1:15-16)

> The saying is sure: If any one aspires to the office of bishop, he desires a noble task. (3:1)

> The saying is sure: If we have died with him, we shall also live with him; if we endure, we shall also reign with him; if we deny him, he also will deny us; if we are faithless, he remains faithful—for he cannot deny himself. (2 Tim 2:11-13)

The only exception appears to be in 1 Timothy 4:9 (The saying is sure and worthy of full acceptance). However, since it repeats verbatim the phraseology of its first occurrence (1:15), after the shorter version in 3:1 (The saying is sure), it is clearly intended to function as a reminder of the content of 1:15-16. Indeed, the

---

[7] See *NTI₁* 177; Dykstra, T., *Mark, Canonizer of Paul: A New Look at Intertextuality in Mark's Gospel* (OCABS Press: St Paul, MN; 2012) 88-89; Adamczewski, B. *The Gospel of Mark: A Hypertextual Commentary* (Peter Lang: Frankfurt am Main; 2014) 94-99.

following verse 4:10 speaks of the salvation wrought through Jesus Christ, which is precisely what the first "saying" (1:15-16) is all about:

> The saying is sure and worthy of full acceptance. For to this end we toil and strive, because we have our hope set on the living God, who is the Savior (*sōtēr*; from the same root as *sōsai*) of all men, especially of *those who believe* (*piston*; from the same root as *pistevein*). (4:9-10)

In Titus, on the other hand, the phrase "the saying is sure" seems to hang in mid-air, unless one considers that it refers to the preceding:

> For we ourselves were once foolish, disobedient, led astray, slaves to various passions and pleasures, passing our days in malice and envy, hated by men and hating one another; but when the goodness and loving kindness of God our Savior appeared, he saved us, not because of deeds done by us in righteousness, but in virtue of his own mercy, by the washing of regeneration and renewal in the Holy Spirit, which he poured out upon us richly through Jesus Christ our Savior, so that we might be justified by his grace and become heirs in hope of eternal life. The saying is sure. (3:3-8)

In any case, its use here is an exception to the rule set in the letters to Timothy. It assumes rather than discloses the content of the "sure (faithful) word (saying)." The reason behind such an approach is found in the first usage of the "sure saying" in Titus. There the bishop is required to "hold firm to the sure (faithful; *pistou*) word (saying; *logou*) *according to the teaching* (*kata tēn didakhēn*; as taught [RSV]), so that he may be able to give instruction (*parakalein*; exhort) in the[8] sound (*hygiainousē*) doctrine (*didaskalia*; teaching) and also to confute those who contradict it." (Tit 1:9). It is clear then that the "sure word

---

[8] The definite article is omitted in RSV.

(saying)" is contained in the "sound teaching" that has already been expounded in 1 and 2 Timothy.⁹

The entire first chapter of Titus revolves around the Pauline gospel. This is confirmed in the last verse of the chapter where the opponents are described in the following way: "They profess to know God, but they deny him by their *deeds* (*ergois*; works); they are detestable, disobedient, unfit *for any (every) good deed* (*pros pan ergon agathon*; all good work)." (v.16a) Twice in the previous letter Paul underscored that "If any one purifies himself from what is ignoble, then he will be a vessel for noble use, consecrated and useful to the master of the house, ready *for any good work* (*eis pan ergon agathon*)" (2 Tim 2:21); "All scripture is inspired by God and profitable for teaching, for reproof, for correction, and for training in righteousness, that the man of God may be complete, equipped *for every good work* (*pros pan ergon agathon*)." (3:16-17). This latter statement sounds as though "good work" is the final aim of the scripture that is inspired by God. In Colossians it is made clear that the purpose of knowledge is not to know God intellectually, but to know his will which dictates that we be fruitful in doing the "good work": "And so, from the day we heard of it, we have not ceased to pray for you, asking that you may be filled with the knowledge of his will in all spiritual wisdom and understanding, *to lead a life worthy of the Lord*, fully pleasing to him, *bearing fruit* (*karpophorountes*) *in every good work* (*en panti*¹⁰ *ergō agathō*) and increasing in the knowledge of God." (1:9-10) The seed of this teaching was planted in Galatians:

> For if any one thinks he is something, when he is nothing, he deceives himself. But let each one test his own *work* (*ergon*), and then his reason to boast will be in himself alone and not in his neighbor. For each man will have to bear his own load ... So then,

---

⁹ See 1 Tim 1:10; 6:3; 2 Tim 1:13; 4:3. Notice how the two instances in each epistle form an *inclusio* that brackets the entire letter.
¹⁰ This is the dative case of *pan* (every, all).

as we have opportunity, let us do *good* (*agathon*) *to all men* (*pros pantas*[11]), *and especially to those who are of the household of faith.* (6:3-5, 10)

The same teaching is magisterially summed up in Ephesians, the letter addressed to the headquarters of the Pauline church and thus to every church in the empire:[12]

> For by grace you have been saved through faith; and this is not your own doing, it is the gift of God—not because of works, lest any man should boast. For we are his workmanship, created in Christ Jesus for good works (*epi ergois agathois*), which God prepared beforehand, *that we should walk in them.* (2:8-10)

So with the intent of chapter 1 having been established, we can safely tackle the last hurdle in it, which is Paul's use of "directed" (*dietaxamēn*; Tit 1:5) when giving a charge to Titus. The verb *diatassein* (direct) occurs solely in conjunction with a senior giving an order to a junior, and thus expresses utter superiority.[13] This explains why, in his epistles, Paul uses this verb to speak of his apostolic and thus authoritative directives to church communities (1 Cor 7:17; 11:34; 16:1). In other instances, he resorts to the classic *parakalein* whose connotation is more of a polite, albeit authoritative, request.[14] The verb *parakalein* is found in 1 and 2 Timothy to speak both of Paul's request to Timothy (1 Tim 1:3; 2:1) and of a request made by a bishop to members of his

---

[11] This is the plural accusative case of *pas*, the masculine of the neuter *pan*. "Men" after "all" is not in the original since *pantas* is the masculine plural and "men" is thus assumed.

[12] A good number of reliable manuscripts omit "in Ephesus" after "to the saints" in Eph 1:1, which is the reading endorsed by RSV: "Paul, an apostle of Christ Jesus by the will of God, to the saints who are also faithful in Christ Jesus."

[13] In the New Testament the ones who issue directives are God (Acts 7:44; 1 Cor 9:14; Gal 3:19), Christ (Mt 11:1; Lk 8:55), Roman authorities (Lk 3:13); the Roman emperor (Acts 18:2), a Roman governor (24:23), a Roman tribune (23:31); a Roman master of the house (Lk 17:9, 10), and Paul (Acts 20:13).

[14] An example of such a request would be when a parent or a teacher says, "I ask that you do this or that."

community (5:1; 6:2; 2 Tim 4:2). It is also used in Titus (1:9;[15] 2:6, 15); thus Timothy and Titus are treated as equals. Given all the preceding, Paul's directive (*diatassein*; Tit 1: 5) to a senior adjutant sounds out of place, and appears as though Paul is treating Titus as a regular member of one of his churches. The best way to explain this "demeaning" of a bishop just assigned to teach the correct message is to hear it against the information in the previous chapter, that is, that Titus deserted Paul (2 Tim 4:10), just as Peter and Barnabas did at Antioch (Gal 2:11-13). By assigning Titus to Crete, Paul is giving him a second chance, however, with a caveat. The Greek *Krētēs* (Crete) is very similar in sound to *kritēs* (judge). So during this second chance, Titus will be under God's watchful eye. And his mission is not going to be easy for the following reasons:

1. There will be no third chance since, at the end of the letter, Paul instructs Titus with these words: "As for a man who is factious, after admonishing him once or twice, have nothing more to do with him, knowing that such a person is perverted and sinful; he is self-condemned." (Tit 3:10-11)

2. Just as Paul did, Titus the Gentile will have to champion Paul's message by refuting the Jewish opponents on the basis on their own scriptures; in other words, by "the gospel of God promised beforehand through his prophets *in the holy scriptures*" (Rom 1:1). That is, to say the least, no easy task! Yet, Paul wants to ensure that in the future when Gentiles endorse his gospel as laid down in the New Testament writings, they would

---

[15] RSV translates *parakalein* into "give instruction."

have first received "teaching" (*didaskalia; didakhē*) from the Old Testament scripture.

3. Finally, Titus may not put forth any excuses, even though "Cretans are always liars, evil beasts, lazy gluttons" (Tit 1:12), a harsh criticism that a Cretan Gentile acting like an Old Testament "prophet" leveled against his own people. Nevertheless, it is "the truthful (faithful) word" that counts and not so much its carrier:

> And whether they hear or refuse to hear (for they are a rebellious house) *they will know that there has been a prophet among them*. And you, son of man, be not afraid of them, nor be afraid of their words, though briers and thorns are with you and you sit upon scorpions; be not afraid of their words, nor be dismayed at their looks, for they are a rebellious house. And you shall speak my words to them, whether they hear or refuse to hear; for they are a rebellious house. (Ezek 2:5-7)

Consequently, for the hearers of the Pastoral Epistles throughout the ages, Titus functions as a testing ground, as the last chance after 1 and 2 Timothy, as the "count of three."

Chapter 2

Vv. 1-15 *¹Σὺ δὲ λάλει ἃ πρέπει τῇ ὑγιαινούσῃ διδασκαλίᾳ. ² πρεσβύτας νηφαλίους εἶναι, σεμνούς, σώφρονας, ὑγιαίνοντας τῇ πίστει, τῇ ἀγάπῃ, τῇ ὑπομονῇ. ³Πρεσβύτιδας ὡσαύτως ἐν καταστήματι ἱεροπρεπεῖς, μὴ διαβόλους μηδὲ οἴνῳ πολλῷ δεδουλωμένας, καλοδιδασκάλους, ⁴ ἵνα σωφρονίζωσι τὰς νέας φιλάνδρους εἶναι, φιλοτέκνους, ⁵ σώφρονας, ἁγνάς, οἰκουργούς, ἀγαθάς, ὑποτασσομένας τοῖς ἰδίοις ἀνδράσιν, ἵνα μὴ ὁ λόγος τοῦ θεοῦ βλασφημῆται. ⁶ Τοὺς νεωτέρους ὡσαύτως παρακάλει σωφρονεῖν· ⁷ περὶ πάντα σεαυτὸν παρεχόμενος τύπον καλῶν ἔργων, ἐν τῇ διδασκαλίᾳ ἀφθορίαν, σεμνότητα, ⁸ λόγον ὑγιῆ ἀκατάγνωστον, ἵνα ὁ ἐξ ἐναντίας ἐντραπῇ μηδὲν ἔχων λέγειν περὶ ἡμῶν φαῦλον. ⁹ Δούλους ἰδίοις δεσπόταις ὑποτάσσεσθαι ἐν πᾶσιν, εὐαρέστους εἶναι, μὴ ἀντιλέγοντας, ¹⁰ μὴ νοσφιζομένους, ἀλλὰ πᾶσαν πίστιν ἐνδεικνυμένους ἀγαθήν, ἵνα τὴν διδασκαλίαν τὴν τοῦ σωτῆρος ἡμῶν θεοῦ κοσμῶσιν ἐν πᾶσιν. ¹¹ Ἐπεφάνη γὰρ ἡ χάρις τοῦ θεοῦ σωτήριος πᾶσιν ἀνθρώποις ¹² παιδεύουσα ἡμᾶς, ἵνα ἀρνησάμενοι τὴν ἀσέβειαν καὶ τὰς κοσμικὰς ἐπιθυμίας σωφρόνως καὶ δικαίως καὶ εὐσεβῶς ζήσωμεν ἐν τῷ νῦν αἰῶνι, ¹³ προσδεχόμενοι τὴν μακαρίαν ἐλπίδα καὶ ἐπιφάνειαν τῆς δόξης τοῦ μεγάλου θεοῦ καὶ σωτῆρος ἡμῶν Ἰησοῦ Χριστοῦ, ¹⁴ ὃς ἔδωκεν ἑαυτὸν ὑπὲρ ἡμῶν ἵνα λυτρώσηται ἡμᾶς ἀπὸ πάσης ἀνομίας καὶ καθαρίσῃ ἑαυτῷ λαὸν περιούσιον, ζηλωτὴν καλῶν ἔργων. ¹⁵ Ταῦτα λάλει καὶ παρακάλει καὶ ἔλεγχε μετὰ πάσης ἐπιταγῆς· μηδείς σου περιφρονείτω.*

¹But as for you, teach what befits sound doctrine. ²Bid the older men be temperate, serious, sensible, sound in faith, in love, and in steadfastness. ³Bid the older women likewise to be reverent in behavior, not to be slanderers or slaves to drink; they are to teach what is good, ⁴and so train the young women to love their husbands and children, ⁵to be sensible, chaste, domestic, kind, and submissive to their husbands, that the word of God may not be discredited.

⁶*Likewise urge the younger men to control themselves.* ⁷*Show yourself in all respects a model of good deeds, and in your teaching show integrity, gravity,* ⁸*and sound speech that cannot be censured, so that an opponent may be put to shame, having nothing evil to say of us.* ⁹*Bid slaves to be submissive to their masters and to give satisfaction in every respect; they are not to be refractory,* ¹⁰*nor to pilfer, but to show entire and true fidelity, so that in everything they may adorn the doctrine of God our Savior.* ¹¹*For the grace of God has appeared for the salvation of all men,* ¹²*training us to renounce irreligion and worldly passions, and to live sober, upright, and godly lives in this world,* ¹³*awaiting our blessed hope, the appearing of the glory of our great God and Savior Jesus Christ,* ¹⁴*who gave himself for us to redeem us from all iniquity and to purify for himself a people of his own who are zealous for good deeds.* ¹⁵*Declare these things; exhort and reprove with all authority. Let no one disregard you.*

Now that Paul established that the "sound teaching"[1] is nothing other than the gospel he has consistently preached, he asks Titus to "teach (*lalei*; speak in a way to share the gospel content)[2] what befits this sound doctrine (*didaskalian*; teaching)" (Tit 2:1). Thereafter, in the rest of the letter, he gives a shortened version of what he has expounded upon in 1 and 2 Timothy, which echoes the entire Pauline corpus. However, his thoughts are not randomly thrown down. Rather his presentation is structured in the following way:

1. Titus 2 contains the "sound teaching" which Titus is asked to *lalein*. The imperative *lalei* brackets the chapter, translated as "teach" in v.1 and "declare"

---

[1] Notice how RSV, in translating here *didaskalia* into "doctrine" rather than "teaching," reflects the pervading "theological" bias toward understanding *pistis* as a "creed" versus its original meaning of "trust" in God that his commandments for us to obey and live by are for our *own* good and ultimate salvation.

[2] This is the verb that Paul uses when referring to his preaching the gospel word.

in v.15. The intention behind this is evident. The verb in its positive connotation occurs only in these two instances in the Pastoral Epistles. The only apparent exception is found in 1 Timothy 5:13 where the verb, in the present participle form, is used to describe an action of speaking that is forbidden: "Besides that, they [young widows] learn to be idlers, gadding about from house to house, and not only idlers but gossips and busybodies, saying (*lalousai*) what they should not."

2. Titus 3:1-7 is a "reminder" (Remind [*Hypomimnēske*] them) that culminates in an appended "The saying is sure" (*Pistos ho logos*; v.8a). Here again the intention is unmistakable, since the only other instance of "remind" (*hypomimnēske*) concludes a teaching that is introduced with "The saying is sure" (*pistos ho logos*): "The saying is sure: If we have died with him, we shall also live with him; if we endure, we shall also reign with him; if we deny him, he also will deny us; if we are faithless, he remains faithful—for he cannot deny himself. Remind them of this." (2 Tim 2:11-14a)

3. A request for insistence on this teaching follows, coupled with a caveat that justifies its emphasis (Tit 3:8-11). This is the only instance of the verb *diabebaiousthai* (insist on; give special emphasis; v.8) being used with a positive connotation in the Pastoral Epistles. In 1 Timothy the verb is used to describe the action of those who are teaching a different "doctrine" (1:3): "Certain persons by swerving from these have wandered away into vain

discussion, desiring to be teachers of the law, without understanding either what they are saying or the things about which *they make assertions* (*diabebaiountai*)." (vv.6-7)

4. Finally, as in the previous two letters, the last passage contains special assignments followed by greetings (Tit 3:12-15).

Worthy of note is that in all four sections (Tit 2; 3:1-7, 8-14, 12-15) one finds reference to either good deeds or the aspect of brotherly love, both of which are at the heart of the Pauline gospel:

> Bid the older men be temperate, serious, sensible, sound in faith, in love, and in steadfastness. Bid the older women likewise to be reverent in behavior, not to be slanderers or slaves to drink; they are to teach what is good, and so train the young women to love their husbands and children, to be sensible, chaste, domestic, kind (*agathas*: good), and submissive to their husbands, that the word of God may not be discredited ... Show yourself in all respects a model of *good deeds*, and in your teaching show integrity, gravity ... [Jesus Christ] who gave himself for us to redeem us from all iniquity and to purify for himself a people of his own who are zealous for *good deeds*. (2:2-5, 7, 14)

> Remind them to be submissive to rulers and authorities, to be obedient, to be ready for any honest work, to speak evil of no one, to avoid quarreling, to be gentle, and to show perfect courtesy (*praytēta*)[3] *toward all men*. (3:1-2)

> I desire you to insist on these things, so that those who have believed in God may be careful to *apply themselves to good deeds*; these are excellent and profitable to men. (v.8)

---

[3] This is one of the facets of love in Galatians 5 and translated there as "gentleness" (v.23).

And let our people learn to *apply themselves to good deeds*, so as to help cases of urgent need, and not to be unfruitful. All who are with me send greetings to you. Greet those who *love* us in the faith. Grace be with you all. (vv.14-15)

Chapter 3

Vv. 1-15 ¹Ὑπομίμνησκε αὐτοὺς ἀρχαῖς ἐξουσίαις ὑποτάσσεσθαι πειθαρχεῖν, πρὸς πᾶν ἔργον ἀγαθὸν ἑτοίμους εἶναι, ² μηδένα βλασφημεῖν, ἀμάχους εἶναι, ἐπιεικεῖς, πᾶσαν ἐνδεικνυμένους πραΰτητα πρὸς πάντας ἀνθρώπους. ³ ἦμεν γάρ ποτε καὶ ἡμεῖς ἀνόητοι, ἀπειθεῖς, πλανώμενοι, δουλεύοντες ἐπιθυμίαις καὶ ἡδοναῖς ποικίλαις, ἐν κακίᾳ καὶ φθόνῳ διάγοντες, στυγητοί, μισοῦντες ἀλλήλους. ⁴ ὅτε δὲ ἡ χρηστότης καὶ ἡ φιλανθρωπία ἐπεφάνη τοῦ σωτῆρος ἡμῶν θεοῦ, ⁵ οὐκ ἐξ ἔργων τῶν ἐν δικαιοσύνῃ ἃ ἐποιήσαμεν ἡμεῖς ἀλλὰ κατὰ τὸ αὐτοῦ ἔλεος ἔσωσεν ἡμᾶς διὰ λουτροῦ παλιγγενεσίας καὶ ἀνακαινώσεως πνεύματος ἁγίου, ⁶ οὗ ἐξέχεεν ἐφ᾽ ἡμᾶς πλουσίως διὰ Ἰησοῦ Χριστοῦ τοῦ σωτῆρος ἡμῶν, ⁷ ἵνα δικαιωθέντες τῇ ἐκείνου χάριτι κληρονόμοι γενηθῶμεν κατ᾽ ἐλπίδα ζωῆς αἰωνίου. ⁸ Πιστὸς ὁ λόγος, καὶ περὶ τούτων βούλομαί σε διαβεβαιοῦσθαι, ἵνα φροντίζωσιν καλῶν ἔργων προΐστασθαι οἱ πεπιστευκότες θεῷ. ταῦτά ἐστιν καλὰ καὶ ὠφέλιμα τοῖς ἀνθρώποις· ⁹ μωρὰς δὲ ζητήσεις καὶ γενεαλογίας καὶ ἔρεις καὶ μάχας νομικὰς περιΐστασο, εἰσὶν γὰρ ἀνωφελεῖς καὶ μάταιοι. ¹⁰ αἱρετικὸν ἄνθρωπον μετὰ μίαν καὶ δευτέραν νουθεσίαν παραιτοῦ, ¹¹ εἰδὼς ὅτι ἐξέστραπται ὁ τοιοῦτος καὶ ἁμαρτάνει, ὢν αὐτοκατάκριτος.¹² Ὅταν πέμψω Ἀρτεμᾶν πρὸς σὲ ἢ Τυχικόν, σπούδασον ἐλθεῖν πρός με εἰς Νικόπολιν, ἐκεῖ γὰρ κέκρικα παραχειμάσαι. ¹³ ζηνᾶν τὸν νομικὸν καὶ Ἀπολλῶν σπουδαίως πρόπεμψον, ἵνα μηδὲν αὐτοῖς λείπῃ. ¹⁴ μανθανέτωσαν δὲ καὶ οἱ ἡμέτεροι καλῶν ἔργων προΐστασθαι εἰς τὰς ἀναγκαίας χρείας, ἵνα μὴ ὦσιν ἄκαρποι.¹⁵ Ἀσπάζονταί σε οἱ μετ᾽ ἐμοῦ πάντες. ἄσπασαι τοὺς φιλοῦντας ἡμᾶς ἐν πίστει. ἡ χάρις μετὰ πάντων ὑμῶν.

¹*Remind them to be submissive to rulers and authorities, to be obedient, to be ready for any honest work,* ²*to speak evil of no one, to avoid quarreling, to be gentle, and to show perfect courtesy toward all men.* ³*For we ourselves were once foolish, disobedient,*

led astray, slaves to various passions and pleasures, passing our days in malice and envy, hated by men and hating one another; ⁴but when the goodness and loving kindness of God our Savior appeared, ⁵he saved us, not because of deeds done by us in righteousness, but in virtue of his own mercy, by the washing of regeneration and renewal in the Holy Spirit, ⁶which he poured out upon us richly through Jesus Christ our Savior, ⁷so that we might be justified by his grace and become heirs in hope of eternal life. ⁸The saying is sure. I desire you to insist on these things, so that those who have believed in God may be careful to apply themselves to good deeds; these are excellent and profitable to men. ⁹But avoid stupid controversies, genealogies, dissensions, and quarrels over the law, for they are unprofitable and futile. ¹⁰As for a man who is factious, after admonishing him once or twice, have nothing more to do with him, ¹¹knowing that such a person is perverted and sinful; he is self-condemned. ¹²When I send Artemas or Tychicus to you, do your best to come to me at Nicopolis, for I have decided to spend the winter there. ¹³Do your best to speed Zenas the lawyer and Apollos on their way; see that they lack nothing. ¹⁴And let our people learn to apply themselves to good deeds, so as to help cases of urgent need, and not to be unfruitful. ¹⁵All who are with me send greetings to you. Greet those who love us in the faith. Grace be with you all.

The last two passages (Tit 3:8-11 and 12-15) form the closing for all three Pastoral Epistles and are magisterially constructed to wrap up, in a few words, the Pauline gospel: the entire Law, and by extension all of the Old Testament, is summed up in the love for the needy neighbor (Rom 13:8-10; Gal 5:13-14). What is immediately and unmistakably noticeable is that both sections are locked together through the repeated verbatim statement "to apply themselves to good deeds" (*kalōn ergōn proistasthai*;[1] Tit 3:8 and 14). In the first case, this statement is immediately followed

---

[1] From the verb *histemi*, with the preposition *pro*.

with a description of the opposite behavior: "*But* avoid (*periistaso*)² stupid controversies (*zēteseis*), genealogies (*genealogias*), dissensions (*ereis*), and quarrels over the law (*makhas nomikas*), for they are unprofitable and futile" (v.9). Notice the crafty word play on the rare verbs from the same root *histēmi*.³ Although the sound of the two prepositions *pro* and *peri* are very close, the connotations are practically in opposition: while *pro* reflects that of "going ahead," *peri* carries that of "going around in circles." The conclusion then is that discussions concerning the Law are both unprofitable and futile since Paul has already solved the matter in Romans and Galatians. Those who have "a morbid craving for controversy (*zēteseis*) and for disputes about words (*logomakhias*), which produce envy, dissension (*eris*), slander, base suspicions" (1 Tim 6:4) "profess to know God, but they deny him by their deeds (*tois ergois*); they are detestable, disobedient, unfit for any good deed (*pan ergon agathon*)" (Tit 1:16). The "good deeds" are specifically aimed at those in need of urgent assistance: "And let our people learn to apply themselves to good deeds, so as to help cases of urgent need." (3:14a) Those who do not abide by this directive will be found "fruitless" (*akarpoi*; v.14b) on judgment day and will end under condemnation (self-condemned; v.11b):

> Likewise, my brethren, you have died to the law through the body of Christ, so that you may belong to another, to him who has been raised from the dead in order that *we may bear fruit* (*karpophorēsōmen*) for God. (Rom 7:4)

> But the fruit (*karpos*) of the Spirit is *love*, joy, peace, patience, kindness, goodness, faithfulness, gentleness, self-control; against such there is no law. (Gal 5:22-23)

---

² From the verb *histemi*, with the preposition *peri*.
³ The first occurs eight times, mainly in the Pastoral Letters (Rom 12:8; 1 Thess 5:12; 1 Tim 3:4, 5, 12; 5:17; Tit 3:8, 14). The second is found only four times, two of which in the Pastoral Letters (Jn 11:42; Acts 25:7; 2 Tim 2:16; Tit 3:9).

> And it is my prayer that your *love* may abound more and more, with knowledge and all discernment, so that you may approve what is excellent, and may be pure and blameless for the day of Christ, filled with the fruits (*karpon*; fruit) of righteousness which come through Jesus Christ, to the glory and praise of God. (Phil 1:9-11)

> Of this you have heard before in the word of the truth, the *gospel* which has come to you, as indeed in the whole world it is *bearing fruit* (*karpophoroumenon*) and growing—so among yourselves, from the day you heard and understood the grace of God in truth, as you learned it from Epaphras our beloved fellow servant. He is a faithful minister of Christ on our behalf and has made known to us your *love* in the Spirit. And so, from the day we heard of it, we have not ceased to pray for you, asking that you may be filled with the knowledge of his will in all spiritual wisdom and understanding, to lead a life worthy of the Lord, fully pleasing to him, *bearing fruit* (*karpophorountes*) in *every good work* (*panti ergō agathō*) and increasing in the knowledge of God. (Col 1:5b-10)

What is interesting regarding the verb *proistasthai*, whose meaning in the middle voice is "apply oneself; put oneself ahead" (Tit 3:8 and 14), is that its active voice *proistēmi* means "stand ahead; stand at the head of; be in the position of leadership," as is evident from all other New Testament instances of that verb, four of which occur in 1 Timothy:

> Having gifts that differ according to the grace given to us, let us use them: if prophecy, in proportion to our faith; if service, in our serving; he who teaches, in his teaching; he who exhorts, in his exhortation; he who contributes, in liberality; he who gives aid, with zeal (*ho proistamenos en spoudē*: he that ruleth, with diligence [KJV]); he who does acts of mercy, with cheerfulness. (Rom 12:6-8)

> But we beseech you, brethren, to respect those who labor among you and *are over* (*proistamenous*) you in the Lord and admonish you. (1 Thess 5:12)
>
> He must *manage* (*proistamenon*; One that ruleth [KJV]) his own household well, keeping his children submissive and respectful in every way; for if a man does not know how to manage (*prostēnai*; rule [KJV]) his own household, how can he care for God's church? ... Let deacons be the husband of one wife, and let them manage (*proistamenoi*; ruling [KJV]) their children and their households well. (1 Tim 3:4-5, 12)
>
> Let the elders who rule (*proestōtes*) well be considered worthy of double honor, especially those who labor in preaching and teaching. (1 Tim 5:17)

The keen ear of someone who knows Greek will have picked up on the inference to Paul's teaching on love in 1 Corinthians. To those graced with the most impressive of spiritual gifts in the church, i.e., the prophets, and those who speak in tongues who are vying to be recognized as the most prominent (1 Cor 12), Paul shows the true way of excellence:

> But earnestly desire the higher gifts. And I will show you a still more excellent way. If I speak in the tongues of men and of angels, but have not love, I am a noisy gong or a clanging cymbal. And if I have prophetic powers, and understand all mysteries and all knowledge, and if I have all faith, so as to remove mountains, but have not love, I am nothing. If I give away all I have, and if I deliver my body to be burned, but have not love, I gain nothing ... Make love your aim, and earnestly desire the spiritual gifts, especially that you may prophesy. (12:31; 13:1-3; 14:1)

What remains to be tackled are the names in Titus 3:12-13 and their function within the context of the text. Firstly, concerning Titus, Paul asks him to hurry and come at Nicopolis before winter (v.12) just as he did Timothy (2 Tim 4:21a); the reason being is that the Lord would soon be coming. The name Nicopolis aptly fits this scenario since it means "City of (the) Victory," and would be an oblique reference to the heavenly Zion.[4] Still Nicopolis bears an extra and important connotation to the ears of the original hearers. Two major events that established Octavian as Augustus Caesar were the battle of Philippi (42 B.C.) and the battle of Actium (31 B.C.). The first battle ended with the victory of Marc Anthony and Octavian over Julius Caesar's assassins, Brutus and Longinus. Many veterans of the losing army decided to settle there, which resulted in the area becoming a Roman colony, *Colonia Victrix Philippensium*. The battle at Actium, which resulted in the final victory of Octavian over the combined forces of Marc Anthony and Cleopatra, took place eleven years later. It is at Actium that the Roman republic essentially turned into the Roman empire. In order to commemorate this momentous victory, Octavian founded a new city near Actium in Epirus that he called Nicopolis, the City of Victory, which would later become the capital of the Roman province Epirus Vetus.

Even a cursive reading of the New Testament will readily show that Philippi has the lion's share when compared to Nicopolis, which occurs only at the end of Titus. Geographically, Philippi is the city where Paul preached the gospel for the first time outside the boundaries of Judaism, and is where his preaching bore fruit:

> Setting sail therefore from Troas, we made a direct voyage to Samothrace, and the following day to Neapolis, and from there to Philippi, which is the leading city of the district of Macedonia, and a Roman colony. We remained in this city some days; and on the sabbath day we went outside the gate to the riverside, where we supposed there was a place of prayer; and we sat down and spoke to the women who had come together. One who heard us was a woman named Lydia, from the city of Thyatira, a seller of purple

---

[4]In discussing Hierapolis (Col 4:13) I have shown that its meaning was "Holy City; City of holiness" and, as such, functioned as a stand-in for the heavenly Jerusalem. See my comments in *C-Col* 100.

goods, who was a worshiper of God. The Lord opened her heart to give heed to what was said by Paul. And when she was baptized, with her household, she besought us, saying, "If you have judged me to be faithful (*pistēn*)[5] to the Lord, come to my house and stay." And she prevailed upon us. (Acts 16:11-15)

Paul may have preached in Philippi first for several reasons: (1) it was part of the land of Alexander who was the first to spread Hellenism (and thus the Gentile way par excellence) widely beyond the borders of classical Greece[6]; (2) it was a Roman colony starting in 42 B.C. and thus a mini-Rome; (3) it was situated on the *Via Egnatia* that linked Asia Minor to Italy.

So from "the first day" the gospel, which is nothing other than the *torah* preached to the nations, was linked to the name of Philippi, as Paul clearly spells out: "And you Philippians yourselves know that *in the beginning of the gospel* (*en arkhē tou evangeliou*),[7] *when I left Macedonia*, no church entered into (table) fellowship[8] (*ekoinōnēsen*) with me in giving and receiving except you only." (4:15) If the "beginning of the gospel" is linked to Paul's leaving Macedonia rather than entering it, this means that the gospel was actually "born" *in* Macedonia when its message was accepted by a few Gentiles who joined in table fellowship with the Jew Paul and his Jewish colleagues. The gospel seed that faltered in Antioch, the "land" of Judaism, bore fruit in the "land" of Philip and Alexander and, by extension, of Augustus Caesar. In other words, Paul planted the seed of Christ, the anti-emperor icon, in the same city where Octavian planted the seed that would become the Roman empire.

---

[5] The feminine of *pistos* whose meaning is "believer; one who trusts."
[6] It was named after Alexander's father, Philip II, who united Macedonia and conquered Illyria, Thrace, and Greece.
[7] Which Mark borrowed as the title of his Gospel.
[8] RSV has "partnership."

Symbolically, Octavian's victory at Actium and the establishment of Nicopolis, the city of his victory, represented his successful unification of the Roman Empire under one administration. Geographically, it constituted a major transportation and communications link between the eastern and western halves of the Mediterranean. Here in Titus, at the end of his odyssey for the gospel's sake (2 Tim 4:6-8), Paul summons Titus (3:12) as well as Timothy (2 Tim 4:21) to join him before winter, and in advance of the return of his victorious Lord, at "his" Nicopolis, the heavenly Zion.

Since the numeral four reflects universality, the four names in Titus 3:12-13 metaphorically represent the full success of the Pauline mission throughout the "four corners" of the Roman empire. This message is further enhanced by the meanings of the names as well as their order (vv.12-13). Titus is not to worry about what will happen to his church in Crete after he has joined Paul in Nicopolis since Paul will send to Crete either Tychicus or Artemas (v.12). Since the Greek *tykhē* means "fate, chance, fortuity," Tychicus (*Tykhikos*) is anyone God may choose, thus indicating that God will remain in control of the situation after the departure of Titus. Moreover, since the Greek adjective *artemēs* means "safe," Paul is reassuring Titus that not only will God keep an eye on the church in Crete, but he will also ensure its safety. The idea of safety is underscored indirectly by the name Artemas which sounds almost like Artemis. The intended assonance finds support in that the goddess Artemis is the twin sister of Apollos whose name is heard in conjunction with Zenas, the fourth name in the series (v.13). The followers of Artemis threatened the lives of Paul and his companions in Ephesus (Acts 19:21-40), the city of "the temple of the great goddess Artemis" (vv.27, 35), and yet Paul's retinue ended up unharmed and "safe." What God performed at Ephesus, where Timothy is bishop, he could easily do in Crete, where Titus is bishop. Consequently, Paul can summon both of them to join him before winter.

If Paul is sending Artemas or Tychicus to Crete, he is conversely asking Titus to speed Paul's way "Zenas the lawyer and Apollos." Paul uses the same phraseology in his appeal to Titus as he did with Timothy:

> When I send Artemas or Tychicus to you, do your best (*spoudason*) to come to me at Nicopolis, for I have decided to spend the winter there. Do your best (*spoudaiōs*) to speed Zenas the lawyer (*nomikos*; person acquainted and dealing with the Law) and Apollos on their way; see that they lack nothing. (Tit 3:12-13)
>
> Do your best (*Spoudason*) to come to me soon ... Do your best (*Spoudason*) to come before winter. (2 Tim 4:9, 21)

The two names, Zenas and Apollos, support the contention that Nicopolis refers to the heavenly Zion. Apollos is Paul's co-adjutant who toiled among the nations by helping Paul water the gospel seed planted in Corinth, the capital of Achaia, the most Greek among the Roman provinces (1 Cor 3:5).[9] Conversely, when one considers that the Greek *Zēnas* is based on the verb *zēn* (live), then *Zenas ho nomikos* sounds to the ear as someone who teaches the divine law as life-giving to both Israel and the nations, which is precisely the situation describing the heavenly Zion:

> It shall come to pass in the latter days that the mountain of the house of the Lord shall be established as the highest of the mountains, and shall be raised above the hills; and all the nations shall flow to it, and many peoples shall come, and say: "Come, let us go up to the mountain of the Lord, to the house of the God of Jacob; that he may teach us his ways and that we may walk in his paths." For out of Zion shall go forth the law, and the word of the Lord from Jerusalem. He shall judge between the nations, and shall decide for many peoples; and they shall beat their swords into plowshares, and their spears into pruning hooks; nation shall not

---

[9] See further Acts 18:24; 19:1; 1 Cor 1:12; 3:4-6, 22; 4:6.

lift up sword against nation, neither shall they learn war any more. (Is 2:2-4)

Further Reading

Commentaries and Studies

Aageson, J. W. *Paul, the Pastoral Epistles, and the Early Church*. Library of Pauline Studies. Peabody, MA: Hendrickson, 2008.

Bénétreau S. *Les épîtres pastorales. 1 et 2 Timothée, Tite*. Commentaire Évangélique de la Bible. Vaux-sur-Seine: ÉDIFAC, 2008.

Collins, R. F. *1 & 2 Timothy and Titus. A Commentary*. New Testament Library. Louisville, KY—London: Westminster John Knox, 2002.

Fiore, B. *The Pastoral Epistles. First Timothy, Second Timothy, Titus*. Sacra Pagina 12. Collegeville, MN: Liturgical, 2009.

Johnson, L. T. *The First and Second Letters to Timothy. A New Translation with Introduction and Commentary*. Anchor Bible 35A. New York—London: Doubleday, 2001.

Krause, D. *1 Timothy*. Readings: A New Biblical Commentary. London—New York: T&T Clark, 2004.

Marshall, I. H. with Towner, P. H. *A Critical and Exegetical Commentary on the Pastoral Epistles*. International Critical Commentary. Edinburgh: T&T Clark, 1999.

Montague, G. T. *First and Second Timothy, Titus*. Catholic Commentary on Sacred Scripture. Grand Rapids: Baker, 2008.

Ngewa, S. M. *1 & 2 Timothy and Titus*. Africa Bible Commentary. Grand Rapids: Zondervan—Hippo Books, 2009.

Towner, P. H. *The Letters to Timothy and Titus*. New International Commentary on the New Testament. Grand Rapids—Cambridge, UK: Eerdmans, 2006.

Stott, J. R. W. *The Message of 1 Timothy and Titus. Guard the Truth*. The Bible Speaks Today. Leicester, UK—Downers Grove, IL: Inter-Varsity, 2001.

Quinn, J. D. and Wacker, W. C. *The First and Second Letters to Timothy. A New Translation with Notes and Commentary.* Eerdmans Critical Commentary. Grand Rapids—Cambridge, UK: Eerdmans, 2000.

Van Neste, R. *Cohesion and Structure in the Pastoral Epistles.* JSNT Supplement Series 280. London—New York: T&T Clark International, 2004.

Wright, N. T. *Paul for Everyone. The Pastoral Letters. 1 & 2 Timothy and Titus.* Louisville, KY: Westminster John Knox, 2004.

Articles

Fitzmyer, J. A. "The Structured Ministry of the Church in the Pastoral Epistles." *Catholic Biblical Quarterly* 66 (4, 04) 582-96.

Häfner, G. "Das Corpus Pastorale als literalisches Konstrukt." *Theologische Quartalschrift* 187 (4, 07) 258-73.

Mappes, D. A. "Moral Virtues Associated with Eldership." *Bibliotheca Sacra* 160 (3, '09) 338-54.

Marshall, J. W. "'I left you in Crete': Narrative Deception and Social Hierarchy in the Letter to Titus." *Journal of Biblical Literature* 127 (638, 03) 202-18.

Stanislas, S. "The *Agōn* of the Servant of Christ in the Pastoral Epistles." *Indian Theological Studies* 47 (1, '10) 73-95.

Wieland, G. M. "Roman Crete and the Letter to Titus." *New Testament Studies* 55 (3, '09) 338-54.

www.ingramcontent.com/pod-product-compliance
Lightning Source LLC
Chambersburg PA
CBHW060523100426
42743CB00009B/1412